Wars End With Me

There's nothing like regret to remind us we're alive.

By Shari L. Berg
with
Patrick Strobel

WARS END WITH ME

For additional information:
Website . . . . . www.warsendwithme.com
Facebook . . . . https://www.facebook.com/warsendwithme/
Twitter . . . . . . https://twitter.com/warsendwithme
To email Shari: thewritereflection@gmail.com

Editor: Peter Bosak, Steel Town Communications
Johnstown, Pa.

Cover Design: Shari L. Berg, The Write Reflection
www.thewritereflection.com

**The cover includes a photo of Patrick Strobel with the vehicle in which he was traveling when his convoy came under attack near Fallujah, Iraq.

Dedication
§

This book is dedicated to my family – who have supported and encouraged me to bring this story to life on the written page – but especially for my father, a veteran of the Vietnam War. I also dedicate it to my son, Connor, and his generation, in the hopes that they will be the ones to find another way, so they will never have to experience the kind of soul-damaging trauma that so many of our soldiers and veterans are living with today.
~Shari

I would like to recognize a few significant people in my life. To my mother Nancy, and wife Donna, your support is abundant, your love is nourishing, and your patience is immeasurable. To my children, Hali and Josh, you have been my beacon of light along a darkened turbulent coast. To the men and women with whom I've served and the dedicated medical personnel who saved my life. And finally, I would like to thank God for sending his warrior Angels to ride shotgun with me on that fateful day.
~Pat

Acknowledgments
§

When we started this book nearly four years ago, we had no idea where the journey would lead us – or that it would take so long to get there. But, like the daily battle our veterans and active military personnel who have been diagnosed with PTSD face, we made the commitment to continue on until every word we wanted to share was included somewhere in the pages of this book.

First and foremost, we would like to thank our families. Our mothers, fathers, siblings, children and spouses have been our biggest cheerleaders throughout this entire process. You have been there for us, encouraging us when we felt like quitting, and supporting our efforts to bring hope to other veterans struggling with PTSD. We love and appreciate each and every one of you.

This book also would not be possible without the assistance and participation of the veterans and medical professionals who agreed to share their stories and their advice to others struggling with PTSD in the pages of this book. Thank you for your bravery and for your honesty in chronicling your ongoing battle with PTSD.

To Dr. Sudip Bose, a heartfelt thank you for not only sharing your efforts to bring awareness to PTSD and abolish the stigma surrounding it, but for continuing to fight for the health and well-being of our veterans. Our readers will want to check out The Battle Continues, Dr. Bose's nonprofit organization that is dedicated to raising awareness and providing assistance to veterans who have returned from war. Information about the organization can be found in the Resources section of this book.

To Kate Dahlstedt, co-founder of Soldier's Heart clinical psychologist, your candidness about women veterans and PTSD is greatly appreciated. Oftentimes, women veterans struggling with PTSD can be overlooked. But the trauma is just as real and devastating for them as it is for their male counterparts. Additionally, your sharing of the Soldier's Heart program protocol for the book is something we especially appreciate, as we feel it is something that truly can make a difference in the lives of those who have picked up this book in their quest to be understood and helped. Information about Soldier's Heart can be found in the Resources section of this book.

To Dr. Roger Brooke, a licensed psychologist and Director of the Military Psychological Services at the Duquesne University Psychology Clinic, thank you for sharing your perspective on how PTSD not only affects the mind, but also the soul. Your words, combined with those of Kate Dahlstedt, provide powerful credence to the belief that PTSD trauma resides not in the mind, but in the soul. It is our hope that your words encourage veterans to consider tackling their PTSD in a way that they may not have previously considered. To Samantha Supernaw, a licensed therapist who shared her successes with a specific form of counseling protocol for individuals with PTSD, thank you for taking the time to share this groundbreaking therapy method with our readers, and for your willingness to continue to hone your skills and expertise so that you may be a resource for our veterans.

To our editor, Peter Bosak, who helped us to bring this manuscript to life in a readable format, thank you for being a part of this journey. Your word-smithing abilities have been truly appreciated.

And lastly, to the veterans and their families who have dedicated their lives in service to this country, we appreciate you the most. We hope those of you who are struggling with PTSD – whether you are an active military member, a veteran or a loved one – find the contents of this book to be helpful to you, providing a sense of peace in knowing that others share in your journey, and the encouragement to continue the battle.

~Shari and Pat

Preface

§

Dear Readers,

First of all, thank you for picking up our book. It truly has been a labor of love for me and Pat and we are glad to finally see it come to fruition.

This book, and its companion website, is intended to serve as a resource for veterans and their families who are battling Post Traumatic Stress Disorder (PTSD). One in every four veterans returning from combat will be diagnosed with PTSD, according to statistics from the U.S. Department of Veterans Affairs.

When I first started to research PTSD, I was overwhelmed by the number of veterans who are dealing with the daily effects of this disorder. The numbers are truly staggering. Among the recent statistics:

•   Twenty percent of veterans who served in Operations Iraqi Freedom and Enduring Freedom have developed PTSD.
•   PTSD affects 12 percent of all veterans who served during the Gulf War.
•   While not widely diagnosed immediately following this service period, as signs of PTSD become more recognizable to medical professionals, more Vietnam veterans are being diagnosed with PTSD as well. Presently, 30 percent of Vietnam veterans have suffered with PTSD at some point post-service.

Given these sobering statistics, it is entirely possible you know a veteran with PTSD. Not all war wounds are visible, and some veterans with PTSD have become quite skilled at hiding their struggle from those around them.

Pat and I met in 2002 when I was a reporter at a daily newspaper in his hometown of Butler, Pa. When Pat deployed to Iraq in February 2003, the newspaper asked me to correspond with him while he was in Iraq, with the intent of chronicling his service. Less than seven months later, I received the call that Pat had been seriously injured when the vehicle in which he was riding came under attack while passing through Fallujah. That moment changed Pat's life not only because of the physical injuries he sustained, but also because of the emotional trauma that he still lives with today. Pat is that one in four veterans who battles daily with PTSD.

When Pat called me and asked me to help him write a book about his PTSD, I was more than happy to assist him in telling his story. Not only did I want to help Pat with his decade-long battle with PTSD – I wanted to make a difference for other veterans who struggle with these same invisible wounds. It is our hope that by telling his story – and the story of others like him – that the stigma attached to veterans suffering with PTSD will be erased and the process toward healing can begin.

Thank you for joining us on our journey.

~Shari

Table of Contents
§

Foreword

§

"I need your help. I have to tell my story. It's the only way I'm going to heal."

Those were the words that Patrick Strobel spoke to me in an air of urgency on the phone one day back in 2013. It had been years since we had spoken; and for that, I felt horrible. I knew Patrick had been diagnosed with Post Traumatic Stress Disorder (PTSD) many years before that, but had not kept in touch with him to see how he was doing. Life, as they say, had gotten in the way. I married, had a child, started my own business and was fully engaged in the stressors of everyday life. I made the age-old mistake of assuming that no news was good news where Patrick was concerned. The reality of his situation could not have been further from that assumption. Patrick had been struggling with his PTSD for nearly a decade at that point, and was desperately searching for something that would help him return to as close to normal as he was ever going to be. Telling his story, according to his psychologist, was a step in that direction.

Patrick turned to me to help with this monumental task be-cause, as he jokingly put it, "Weapons I know, but writing is not my thing." The thought of putting together his story in a way that would make others want to share in it just added to his stress. So, he reached out to me in the hopes that I'd be willing to assist. He didn't choose me at random for the job of telling the story of his struggles. He chose me because I had a history of telling his story.

Patrick and I met in 2002 when I was a journalist at his hometown newspaper. Less than a year later, he told me he was deploying to

Iraq to serve in the Iraqi Freedom campaign launched by then-President George W. Bush. My editor saw an opportunity to report, so to speak, from the front lines and asked me to write about Patrick's service while he was deployed. As often as he was able to check in from the front lines, I would produce an accounting of what it was like to be Patrick, living and serving his country in an active war zone. Among other things, I wrote about a (literal) monkey on his back, what it was like to try to perform basic hygiene in an active war zone and the creative ways soldiers learned to sleep on the battlefield. Seven months after his deployment, I also had the disheartening task of reporting on the attack on his convoy, which left him with life-threatening injuries and the PTSD he is still battling to this day.

When I agreed to help Patrick with his request to continue telling his story a decade after I'd last reported on it, I had no idea how huge of an undertaking it would prove. Writing a book is not the same as writing a series of feature or news stories. It is a lot more involved in many respects. Never one to turn down a challenge, though, I rolled up my sleeves and delved into the unknown.

During the planning phase, Patrick and I agreed that in addition to telling his story, we wanted to offer the same opportunity to other veterans he knew who were sharing in the struggle of living with PTSD. You will meet some of these brave men and women in the pages of this book. And while we only provide a glimpse into their daily lives and their ongoing battle with PTSD, we give them our heartfelt gratitude for being willing to open up and share their experiences in the hope that it may help another veteran with PTSD. Part I and portions of Part II of this book are dedicated to sharing

Patrick's story and those of other veterans. From a storyteller's perspective, I will share that it was very emotionally draining to listen to the struggles of these men and women. There were times I had to walk away from this book for a few days or weeks in order to regain my composure, and other times I would just sit and cry after hearing about the trauma they endured that later resulted in the development of their PTSD. There were also days that I decided I couldn't bear to hear one more story of war trauma, because it was taking such an emotional toll on me. I would proclaim loudly to anyone who had the misfortune of being within ear-shot that I was done, that I wasn't going to finish this book. But then I reminded myself that I had the leisure of closing the proverbial book and walking away; veterans and their families who are living with the lasting effects of PTSD do not have that option. So, I dusted myself off and dove back in with newfound determination to do Patrick's story justice. If you've never listened to a veteran tell the story of war, I believe it's something every citizen of this country should do (and is some-thing we address in Chapter 11 of this book). It provides a whole new perspective on the horror of war, which is something that most of us (thankfully) never have to experience personally. But I wholeheartedly believe it is our duty to share that burden with the men and women who have placed themselves on the front lines in service to our country.

In addition to sharing their stories, Patrick and I also felt it was important to briefly address the history of PTSD and its clinical definition, which we do in Parts I and II. As a caveat, I am not a medical professional by trade, nor do I play one on TV. The sections of our book which address the clinical and historical sides of PTSD are not as in-depth as some other PTSD books on the market, and are written in a way that the average reader can understand, not using language and terminology more readily found in scientific research and professional journals. We have recommended a few of the more in-depth books in our resource section, so if you are looking for something that will delve more into the clinical side of PTSD, you have some options to explore.

Additionally, Part II discusses the stigma that surrounds PTSD for veterans and active military personnel who are diagnosed with the condition, and what can be done to combat it. Our thanks to Dr. Sudip Bose for agreeing to be a part of our story. Dr. Bose has dedicated his life to veteran advocacy, using his combined experience as a veteran and a medical professional to increase access and improve the quality of care our veterans receive. As part of his mission, Dr. Bose created the nonprofit organization *The Battle Continues*, with the goal of raising awareness and helping veterans returning from war. Hear more about what Dr. Bose has to say about PTSD stigma and veteran advocacy in Chapter 5.

We also felt it was important to provide our readers with resources. There is no shortage of books on the market today that spend hundreds of pages talking about the clinical side of PTSD, or offer brutal – and sometimes depressing – testimonials of what it is like to live with PTSD. We didn't want to be another one of those books. We didn't want our readers to finish this book so depressed that they felt their battle with PTSD was hopeless. It is why Section III of our book is dedicated to talking about the traditional and non-traditional ways some veterans have found relief for their everyday struggles with PTSD. Thank you to Dr. Roger Brooke, Kate Dahlstedt and Samantha Supernaw for sharing their expertise with our readers. It is our profound hope that by offering examples of what has worked – or not worked – for others, that our readers will finish this book with a newfound determination to continue fighting, as well as peace in knowing that their battle with PTSD is not lost.

Section I
Invisible Wounds, Deep Scars

****

"It is the soldier, not the reporter, who has given us freedom of the press. It is the soldier, not the poet, who has given us freedom of speech. It is the soldier, not the campus organizer, who has given us the freedom to demonstrate. It is the soldier, who salutes the flag, who serves beneath the flag, and whose coffin is draped by the flag, who allows the protester to burn the flag."
~Father Dennis Edward O'Brien, USMC

****

CHAPTER ONE
Regrets
§

"If only. Those must be the two saddest words in the world."
~Mercedes Lackey

There's nothing like regret to remind us we're alive.

Some people regret wasting their youth in the pursuit of foolish things, while others lament over a lost relationship. Some people look back and wish they had had more fun in life or had crossed more items off their bucket lists.

Everyone has something they regret, and each person has their own definition of regret. The Merriam-Webster Dictionary defines regret as feeling sad or sorry about something that you did or did not do. If only it were that simple.

Patrick Strobel's definition of regret is more complex. Regret is the thing that keeps him up at night. It's the thing that fuels his anger and sadness, and the thing that on some days, consumes him whole.

If only.

Patrick says those two words a lot when talking about Aug. 12, 2003. If only he hadn't allowed Sgt. Williams to come that day. "I warned him how dangerous being in one of my convoys could be, but he insisted on coming. Our convoy was making a supply-refresher run from our base to one near Ramadi where his wife was stationed. Sgt. Williams didn't want to miss out on an opportunity to see his wife. I let my emotions cloud my judgment, knowing that if our roles were reversed, I'd want the opportunity to see my wife. Looking back now, I wish I had been more forceful about not allowing him to come."

Giving in and allowing Sgt. Williams to come is only part of his endless torment. If only he had insisted Sgt. Williams sit directly behind the driver instead of letting him sit in the back, he might still be alive. "I knew the safest place in the soft-top vehicles we were still driving back then was directly behind the driver. But that's not where Sgt. Williams sat. He insisted on sitting in the back – a place where I normally would be seated," Patrick recalled, his voice becoming softer with each word. "That's my biggest regret and the one 'what if' I focus on a lot. It's the one that hurts me the most because it should have been me, not him. I should be the one who died that day."

The guilt Patrick feels over the death of Sgt. Williams is only a small piece of the complex puzzle that created his ongoing battle with PTSD.

I was in a five-vehicle convoy on a supply-refresher trip to a base near Ramadi. It was a trip I'd made many times and we knew it would take us a good four hours to do it. Our goal when we set out that day was to get back before dark. It's a pretty intense trip, because you are in an area where you can take an ambush or enemy fire pretty much the entire time. I had all of the radio frequencies for every base along the way memorized so I could call for help to the nearest one if we came under attack. I had just started thinking that it was strange because it was normally a very busy highway. Then we got hit. I was told later we had run over an IED (improvised explosive device). When it happened, I didn't feel any pain. All I saw was how bright everything was, and I remember thinking things but I couldn't get them out. I couldn't move. My ears were ringing and I kept thinking, 'No way did that just happen. Holy shit, I just died in Iraq.'

Normally IED explosions are followed by small arms fire, but I couldn't hear anything except the ringing in my ears. That's when I started to think about my family – how I was going to die right there and never see them again – and that's when I started to see colors and shapes adjusting and, before I knew it, I was overwhelmed by intense physical pain. It hurt, but I knew if I felt it, I must still be alive.

The excitement of being alive quickly faded, though, as the pain became more intense. That pain was so overwhelming. I looked down and realized that my arm was on fire and had hanging, burnt skin on it. It was mangled and I couldn't move it. I became aware of the pain in my leg next. I realized the heater core had been destroyed during the explosion, and antifreeze was pouring onto me. I could see Jake, the driver, was unconscious, but Sgt. Williams was gone. He wasn't even in the vehicle anymore. I don't know how long we traveled like that – with both of us unconscious. I had shrapnel in my back from my canteen, which burst on impact during the explosion. I knew I was in bad shape. When Jake finally came to, he managed to pull over.

But I knew we weren't out of danger, and that's when I started to assess myself to see if I had any whoop ass still left in me. I quickly decided that I didn't think I did. I knew I was combat disabled, which was scary, because I could see 12 to 15 Iraqi men approaching us and I really thought that was it. I managed to get out of the vehicle, but when I tried to stand up, I realized I had a piece of metal protruding from my leg and that my leg was likely broken. When I realized I couldn't do anything for myself, I just wanted to crawl into a hole. I couldn't even stand up. How was I going to defend myself?

I found out later that one of the other vehicles from our convoy that wasn't hit during the initial explosion decided not to stop to help us. They kept on going because they didn't want to deal with the crowd of Iraqis that was gathering so they just left us there, me and Jake. That was the worst feeling in the world to know we'd been abandoned like that. I figured I'd survived the initial attack, only to die at the hands of this crowd of Iraqi men who were fast approaching us.

I don't know how he did it, but Jake managed to pull a weapon and focus it on the approaching men. Then I noticed a cab heading down the road behind us, and it was full of Iraqi men. I remember telling Jake if the cab kept coming, to shoot the driver. But at the last minute, they turned off and headed in the other direction. I was relieved, but I knew we still had to contend with the men who were gathering outside of our vehicle, and I kept wondering when or if help was ever going to arrive. There was an old Iraqi man who was touching his heart and looking at me, and I knew that what he was doing was a sign of respect. He was really getting in my face, though, which made me nervous. But I think he was just trying to get himself between me and the approaching Iraqi men so he could protect me. He's probably the only reason I'm still alive. All I know is that twice within probably 10 minutes, I had made my peace with God, sure I was about to die. About 25 minutes into the situation, another convoy came in. They told me they had recovered Sgt. Williams' body. He didn't make it. They got me and Jake into a vehicle and said they had to get us to a Medevac site. I was scared to death, worrying we would hit other IEDs that might have been planted along that road on our way to the Medevac site.

REGRETS

When I got to Medevac, I saw Sgt. Williams' body, which brought on an intense feeling of survivor's guilt. That guilt has stayed with me a long time. I should have made him sit behind the driver. I just wish it had been different. I tried to talk to his wife, to tell her how sorry I am. But she wouldn't even talk to me, and that really hurt. It only makes my guilt that much worse to not be able to talk to her. To this day, I've still not talked to her and have accepted that I probably never will. I just wanted her to know that in his last moments, he was thinking of her.

Patrick suffered serious injuries in the attack. He required three surgeries on his hand, but has never fully regained feeling or control of his pinky finger. His leg was broken and he had burns from where the heater core antifreeze had leaked onto him. He had shrapnel in his back and shoulder. His hearing also was damaged during the explosion, which causes a constant ringing in his ears and requires the use of hearing aids. Sometimes using white noise will help distract him from the ringing – but only sometimes. "That ringing brings me back to that event," Patrick said. "I think about that event at least three times a day, every day."

There are many things – everyday, ordinary occurrences – that force Patrick crashing back to the events of that day and the feelings of helplessness and frustration that come with it. Sometimes it's just a loud noise he wasn't expecting. Other times, it may be visiting a crowded, public place that sets off his panic button. Patrick has learned over the years how to avoid most of his triggers by simply skipping out on certain events and opportunities, like attending a music concert or sporting event with his family.

But one trigger Patrick hasn't been able to avoid – and which has caused his PTSD to resurface with a vengeance – came in the form of news from his son, Josh. "He just came home one day and told me that he wanted to enlist," said Patrick. "He wants to carry on the Strobel family tradition of serving in the military. His focus is on the medals and the welcome home parades, and I'm not sure he's thinking about the bad things that can come along with serving your country. When he first told me, my immediate response was 'wars end with me,' but he isn't listening. He's old enough to enlist and I know there isn't anything I can do to stop him."

Josh admits that he knows his enlistment is hard on his dad but is firm in his convictions about serving his country. "He was shocked when I told him," Josh recalled. "Once he realized I wasn't going to change my mind, he said he would support me in any way that he could."

Patrick said once he realized there was no talking his son out of it, he had to come to terms with it, even if he still didn't like it. Patrick helped his son study for the ASVAB – a multiple-aptitude battery test administered by the military that is designed to measure developed abilities and predict future academic and occupational success in the military – and spent countless hours talking to him about both the benefits and drawbacks of the military life. Among the drawbacks discussed was the risk for developing PTSD or experiencing other traumatic injuries.

Josh said while he understands that being injured is always a possibility when serving, it is something he chooses not to dwell on. "When my dad got blown up, it's always been a goal for me to join the military and finish what he started," Josh said. "There's always the possibility for me to get injured like my dad, but the way I see it is that I'll be serving this country."

Pictured Above: This is what is left of the humvee Strobel was traveling in when his convoy was hit by the IED.

CHAPTER TWO
All in the Family
§

"A man can't eat anger for breakfast and sleep with it at night and not suffer damage to his soul."
~ Garrison Keillor

Patrick can hardly blame his son for his determination to join the Army. Serving their country is just something the Strobels do.

"We have had a relative on one side or the other in every war we've had in the U.S.," said Nancy Lambert, Patrick's mother. "Patrick heard these stories as a child growing up. It was all the older men talked about."

On both sides of his family of origin, Patrick can trace his family's military service as far back as the French and Indian War. William Brikell – a beaver trapper – fought alongside General Edward Braddock at the Point in what is now modern-day downtown Pittsburgh.

Another family member, William Spencer, served during the Civil War. He signed up for the war when he was under age by stealing his brother's birth certificate. He was only 14 when he served as a drummer boy. Spencer was captured and kept as a prisoner of war in Libby Prison in Virginia, where he lost one of his legs. He spent a year as a P.O.W. before he finally was traded as part of a prisoner exchange.

During World War I, Michael Griffin, a great uncle of Patrick's, served briefly in France, and during World War II, two family members served: Col. Thomas J. Kane and Patrick's grandfather, Paul Strobel.

Col. Kane was part of the U.S. Army Ordnance Bomb Disposal service branch, a group of elite Army Ordnance soldiers, who were the forerunners of today's Explosive Ordnance Disposal branch. Col. Kane, along with eight other American soldiers, traveled to England shortly after the attack on Pearl Harbor to learn about bomb disposal methods from the British. The Brits were credited with having the most advanced bomb disposal program at that time.

Col. Kane and seven other U.S. soldiers graduated from the Royal Engineer Bomb Disposal training course. They returned to the U.S. in early 1942, where they supervised the U.S. Army's first explosive ordnance disposal school, located at Aberdeen Proving Ground in Maryland. The experience was recounted in *Nine From Aberdeen* by Jeffrey M. Leatherwood.

Patrick's grandfather, Paul Strobel Sr., also served in World War II. He started out in the Navy and eventually ended up in the Marines.

Paul was taken prisoner by the Germans during the Battle of the Bulge. His wife, Genevieve, received this notice via Western Union about the status of her husband, who was considered missing in action at the time:

```
41
W1


1                        "WESTERN UNION"
    GA14 GOVT=WASHINGTON DC  12 311 A     1945       JAN.12,1942  7
AM.              MRS.GENEVIEVE STROBEL
                 405 WALKER,AVE.BUTLER,PENN.
        THE SECRETARY OF WAR DESIRES ME TO EXPRESS HIS  DEEP
REGRET
        THAT YOUR HUSBAND PRIVATE FIRST CLASS,PAUL A.STROBEL,SR.HAS
        BEEN REPORTED MISSING IN ACTION SINCE TWENTY ONE DECEMBER
        IN GERMANY.IF FURTHER DETAILS OR OTHER INFORMATION ARE
        RECEIVED YOU WILL BE PROMPTLY NOTIFIED=
        DUNLOP ACTING THE ADJUTANT GENERAL.
```

During the first Gulf War, an Iraqi missile destroyed a barracks that housed more than 100 American troops on Feb. 25, 1991. The attack killed 27 and wounded another 98 soldiers, all of whom served with the 475th Quartermaster Detachment Group, an Army Reserve unit based in Farrell, Pa.

Following that attack, Paul noted that he began having trouble sleeping at night, having nightmares filled with memories of his days as a P.O.W. He would have flashbacks of the hardships he and his fellow prisoners endured. In addition to his service to his country, Paul also had another thing in common with his grandson, Patrick – he battled PTSD.

As a way to deal with the nightmares and flashbacks, Paul began to recount some of his experiences for his family in a series of letters.

Those letters include painful details of his capture in 1942 and his subsequent imprisonment.

We were bombed by the R.A.F. early in the morning doing an air strike against a large railroad yard just outside of our prison. The R.A.F. dropped some of their bombs too soon, hitting our prison, killing several hundred American offi-cers and soldiers. I was going to the rest room to relieve myself when the bombs fell. The concussion of the bombs blew me back where I was sleeping with my buddy, only to find him all blowed to pieces. I shall never forget what used to be a human being. This is why after seeing the killing of those soldiers by that scud missile; I now have trouble sleeping at night. I had a dream that I had a split second to wake up or I shall die. My going to the restroom to relieve myself saved my life. My buddy was killed where I was sleeping beside him.

Paul goes on in his letters to recount that he and his fellow P.O.W.s were forced to work from dawn to dusk and were only fed one meal a day, mostly consisting of bread and water. He weighed 190 when he was first captured, and within the first month, was down to 100 pounds. He had been shot in his lower back, legs and lower stomach, and the wounds developed gangrene. The Germans had an English doctor who also was a P.O.W. operate on his wounds; although the procedure was done without the benefit of anesthesia or anything for the pain.

For six long pages, Paul recounts the horrors of being held as a P.O.W. and the ongoing regret that he wasn't able to do more to end his misery and the misery of his fellow P.O.W.s.

I wish at the time I had a chance to prove myself and be a hero or made a name for myself and came home an honorable soldier instead of a P.O.W. At the time, I was ashamed of myself. You see, I felt I let myself down. I didn't want it this way and I am sorry it happened. I was just 23 years old and to come out of this as a P.O.W. was not my way of coming home. Now you see why it is so hard to write about it. I must stop for now as I cannot control my emotions and I cannot see to write.

After eight long months of what Paul described as a fate worse than death, Russian soldiers fighting with the Allied Forces overtook the camp and set the prisoners free. Once he came home, the shame he already felt for being a P.O.W. hit him even harder after an encounter with another soldier.

When I got discharged after the war, I had a soldier tell me that I was a coward for surrendering to the Germans. Well, when you got the German Army shooting at you point blank with 88's anti-air guns, cannons, machine guns and screaming mee-mees trying to kill you, then only a fool of a man would die. I felt bad about this for a long time and kept this to myself. I would rather be a live coward than a dead hero. This soldier died a drunkard bum whereas I raised eight children (one dead) and worked at Armco for 40 years and made a man out of myself that I am proud of, not a dead hero.

The Strobel family history of service to the country during wartime did not end with Paul. Three uncles served in the Vietnam Conflict, and another in the Korean War.

Patrick himself then entered the fray, enlisting in the U.S. Army in 1988. Fresh out of high school, Patrick noted his options were few and far between if he wanted to be able to support himself and his high-school sweetheart, Donna, whom he wanted to marry. "In Butler (Pa.), there weren't a lot of jobs. So, I was looking for something to give me some extra money so I could get married and start a family."

The Army seemed like a natural choice given his family's history of service.

Patrick received basic training at Fort Dix in New Jersey. He then was sent to Aberdeen Proving Ground in Maryland for five months to receive advanced training. Following training, he was stationed in Germany, where he would spend the next five years. After his first year in Germany, he and Donna married.

It wasn't until Operation Desert Shield/Storm in Iraq in 1991 as part of the first Gulf War that Patrick experienced his first war-time service to his country. Donna went back to Butler to stay with family during his deployment. They both returned to Germany for a year following the first Gulf War before heading to Fort Irwin, Calif., in 1993.

In 1997, Patrick returned to Aberdeen Proving Grounds and, in 1999, he was solicited for warrant officer training, which sent him to Alabama for six weeks of very intensive training. Following training, he ended up back in Fort Irwin and then two years later, was stationed in South Korea. "My wife wasn't allowed to go with me (to South Korea) since it was still considered a hostile zone, so she went to live with my mom in Butler (Pa.)."

In early 2003, Patrick and Donna were sent to Fort Carson, Colo., with the 3rd Armored Cavalry Regiment. Shortly thereafter, Patrick was deployed to Iraq as part of the second Gulf War – the war in which he sustained the injuries that led to his PTSD.

His service didn't end with his injury in Iraq. In 2005 and again in 2006, Patrick was sent back to Iraq, and he then served in Afghanistan for a year, from 2007-2008. Before leaving for Iraq the second time, Patrick was fearful about many things, including being sent back into a war zone, knowing that he was still struggling. He also was afraid that being back in those conditions could cause a further wedge between him and his family members, especially his wife. Before leaving, he wrote the following letter to his wife:

Donna,

I just wanted to let you know how much I appreciate your efforts and sacrifices; some getting little appreciation, and others hardly getting any recognition.

My professional success as a Leader, Warrant Officer, Solider, are directly attributed to your hard work as a mother, domestic manager, and wife. My on-going battles in my recovery efforts, and reason I still wear the uniform today, is due largely to the strong foundation of will and determination that you've instilled in me and our family.

Approximately 15 months ago, I'd almost given up on my professional career in the military. You stood solidly beside me, not pushing me in either direction. You let me process all of my emotions and lent me your ear when I needed to vent. Because of your continued support I am able to continue my service to our country and our Army.

The road to recovery, both mentally and physically, has been longer than any of us imagined. I only hope that the end is near, and we can get on with our lives both personally and professionally. I am certain God has a path for us and will guide us through these challenging times.

In closing, I want to sincerely thank you for your love and devotion. I'm extremely grateful to have you in my life and I look forward to forever with you.

In Afghanistan, Patrick continued to be exposed to the kind of experiences that only served to worsen his PTSD. Patrick was assigned to the unit that served as a support for the Second Platoon, B Company, 2nd Battalion, 503rd Infantry Regiment, 173rd Airborne Brigade Combat Team of the U.S. Army in the Korangal Valley. The platoon was featured in the documentary Restrepo. "Those guys were in the Wild, Wild West. I used to go out to fix their weapons. At one point, I lived with them for about a week and a half."

One of his assignments with the 173rd was to find a way to camouflage their weapons. The weapons were black, and the Taliban fighters easily could spot them in their home environment. So, Patrick designed a camouflage for the weapons and other tools – including helmets – that made it harder for the Taliban to identify and target them.

While he saw some pretty horrific things in Afghanistan, Patrick said he preferred his time there than his time in Iraq. "In Iraq, it was open, and in Afghanistan, it was mountainous and a lot more dangerous. The terrain was so different. In Afghanistan, you could at least find the beauty there." In the years between his service in Iraq and Afghanistan, technology and tools and even weaponry improved, including ways to detect the kind of IEDs that contributed to his attack in Iraq.

But despite the advancements, it was still an experience Patrick said he wished he didn't have to live through — and certainly one he would like to spare his son. But Patrick said his son is so enthralled by the family history in the military that he is letting it cloud his judgment. "He focuses on the medals and the welcome home parades, but he's never experienced anything traumatic. He thinks he's invincible, but I know better. I don't want him to end up like me, battling the flashbacks and the guilt and the rage for the rest of his life."

Josh Strobel left for basic training on Tuesday, July 21, 2015. His decision to join the military was only strengthened during his time at basic training, although he struggled a bit during the first weeks in basic training, turning to his dad for help. "I think he was waiting for me to say, 'I told you so,' but I didn't do that. The first time he called, I think he was looking for permission to quit. He was telling me that he had made a mistake. Even though it was hard for me, I encouraged him instead with a little tough love. I told him he didn't have permission to come home. I told him that once he starts something, he has to complete it."

Patrick also reached out to Josh's first officer and let him know that his son may need some extra guidance and support, which was provided. The interventions helped change Josh's outlook on basic training, which he completed in November 2015. Josh Strobel currently is stationed in the Middle East.

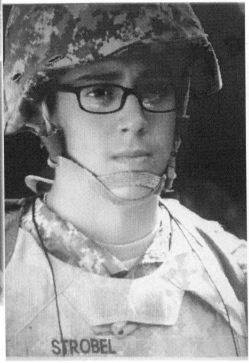

CHAPTER THREE
Hell on Earth

§

"Trauma is hell on earth. Trauma resolved is a gift from the gods."
~Peter A. Levine

Post Traumatic Stress Disorder, more commonly known as PTSD, is hardly a new condition. Following World War I, it was known as shell shock. After World War II, it picked up a new name – battle fatigue. By the time the Vietnam Conflict rolled around, it had changed its name yet again. We discuss the evolution of PTSD further in Chapter 8. Although it is not new regardless of the name it has been given, PTSD has received more attention in recent years due to the staggering number of soldiers being diagnosed with the condition upon their return home from active duty.

According to the U.S. Department of Veterans Affairs, 20 per-cent of veterans who served in Operation Iraqi Freedom and Enduring Freedom have developed PTSD. The condition also affects 12 percent of all veterans who served during the first Gulf War. Presently, 30 percent of Vietnam veterans have been diagnosed with the condition as well. However, PTSD is not exclusive to veterans. Anyone who has suffered a traumatic experience – including victims of violent crime and natural disasters – can struggle with PTSD.

So, what exactly is PTSD?

According to the National Institutes of Health, PTSD can develop following a traumatic or terrifying experience which either resulted in actual physical harm or the threat of physical harm. The human body is designed to react to fear in what is commonly referred to as the fight-or-flight mode. It is a normal, healthy reaction that is designed to protect the body by telling us to either run away or stand up and fight. In a person who develops PTSD, that reaction is altered or damaged, causing them to feel stressed or frightened even when they are not in a dangerous situation. For instance, something as ordinary as a car door slamming shut can trigger stress and fear in someone with PTSD.

Although PTSD is a very real condition, it can be difficult to diagnose. According to the PTSD Alliance, up to 10 percent of Americans will experience PTSD at some point in their lives, which accounts for 30 percent of all victims of trauma. The alliance cites the following medical criteria for medical professionals assessing a patient for the presence of PTSD:

• The person must have witnessed, experienced or learned about a traumatic event in which death or physical harm was threatened;

• The person must re-experience the trauma in their daily life through a number of ways, including nightmares, intrusive thoughts and flashbacks;

• The person chooses a coping mechanism such as avoidance of certain situations or stimuli that may trigger the memories and detaching themselves from relationships and social activities;

• The person must suffer from a heightened arousal, including insomnia, anger, hyper-vigilance or is easily startled; and

• The person must have suffered with these symptoms for a set period of time and is unable to move past them without intervention.

PTSD also affects men and women differently, further complicating diagnosis and treatment outcomes. According to the National Center for PTSD, while women and men report the same symptoms of PTSD – hyperarousal, re-experiencing, avoidance and numbing – some symptoms are more common for women. It is more common for women to blame themselves for the trauma that led to their PTSD than men. Women also are far more likely to experience issues feeling emotions and to avoid things that remind them of the trauma than men.

Another problem with accurately diagnosing PTSD is that many veterans and active military members go to great lengths to hide the fact they are dealing with the disorder. Many feel they are able to manage their symptoms and do not need outside help.

Patrick acknowledged that when he first was seeking treatment for his PTSD, he was embarrassed to admit it and went out of his way to conceal it. When he went to see a psychologist at the Veterans Administration hospital, he deliberately dressed himself in civilian clothing so that no one would know he was in the military, let alone the fact that he had the rank of a commanding officer. He fought the process of obtaining disability for his PTSD once diagnosed, because to do so would be to admit that something was wrong with him.

"Any time I went to see my VA shrink, I would dress in civilian clothes," Patrick admitted sheepishly. "I was a leader in my cavalry, and leaders don't like to admit they have weaknesses. This is definitely a weakness."

Patrick isn't the only veteran with the notion that it's a shameful affair to admit that he has PTSD.

Steve Montelione, a veteran and founder of It's About the Warrior Foundation in Pittsburgh, Pa., said he sees the same denial of the condition for the exact same reasons in many of the veterans his organization assists.

"Some of it has to do with the age of these guys," said Montelione. "The Vietnam Vets will come to me and they will admit they have (PTSD). The younger guys are convinced they're too tough to have it or need help for it."

One of the services offered through It's About the Warrior Foundation is free psychological counseling. "We have an endowment set aside for vets who need counseling but can't afford it."

Denying the existence of PTSD is not always about pride or thinking oneself invincible. Janine Madrid, whose husband Joe was diagnosed with PTSD after returning from combat, said those who are still enlisted have to worry about losing their clearances and even their livelihood if they are deemed mentally unfit for service.

"Men have been taught not to cry, to compartmentalize every-thing and not admit they need help," she said. "These guys build up a façade and heaven forbid anyone see the crap through that façade."

Joe Madrid said it has been an uphill battle for him in dealing with his PTSD, and he wants fellow veterans who are fighting the same battle to know that it is OK to admit you need help and it is OK to cry. "Soldiers tend to push down their feelings so much – because it's what we're taught to do – but they will eventually explode and do something stupid. I want them to know they don't have to hold it all in. It's OK to admit you need help. It's OK to cry. It's OK to be in touch with your feelings and be vulnerable and it's definitely OK to talk about it."

John Vaughn, a retired U.S. Marine with 22 years of service, agreed. Vaughn has been friends with the Strobels for over a decade and said that during the initial years after Pat's injury in Iraq, he spent many nights talking him through PTSD episodes. "What happened to Pat, how he was injured, I just don't think there ever is a normal after something like that. Pat was angry a lot after that, and he really had issues with trust, and I can't say I blame him given the circumstances."

Vaughn said compassion and understanding from friends and family members is necessary in helping veterans to not only admit they have PTSD and need to seek treatment, but in also helping them to cope with it after they are diagnosed. While Vaughn has not officially been diagnosed with PTSD, he said he can relate to his fellow combat soldiers who have been diagnosed. "I don't believe I have PTSD the way some of these guys do, but I do find that I am not as tolerant of people and situations as I was before my time in Iraq in 2004. I can go from zero to pissed off in no time now. There are some people I avoid interacting with now because I know they will do something to push my buttons."

One of Vaughn's biggest triggers is the attitude some people have toward servicemen and women who were deployed during the most recent Iraq and Afghanistan wars, or those who take for granted the freedom that he and others in the military have fought and died to ensure. "It is the disrespect for the men and women who served and blaming them for a war they didn't ask to fight, that really bothers me."

The hardest thing for any soldier to deal with is the transition from military life to civilian life, Vaughn added, which is a process that is made even more difficult for those who also are dealing with PTSD. The lack of structure that is common to life as a civilian is a foreign concept to members of the military. One of the best things veterans with PTSD can do is to find a friend or family member who is willing to help them keep their emotions in check. For Vaughn, that person is his son. "I've told him that if I'm mad for no reason, he needs to tell me, so I can get myself under control."

Family and friends also can help veterans who are having trouble readjusting to civilian life while coping with PTSD by encouraging them to get counseling and to consider attending counseling with them. "It's especially important for kids to get counseling to help them cope with the changes that have occurred in their dad or mom," Vaughn said.

Angel Mojica, a U.S. Marine who served in Iraq, said it was his wife who urged him to seek help after he returned from his second deployment in 2007. "I knew something wasn't right. I wasn't sleeping, and I was self-medicating with liquor a lot. I had intrusive thoughts and nightmares. My wife was the one who prompted me to get help. She knew something wasn't right and she kept encouraging me until I sought help. I swallowed my pride and did what I needed to do."

Mojica sought individual and group counseling, and is on medication to control some of his symptoms. He and his wife also attend marriage/couples therapy together. Learn more about what has and hasn't worked for him and his family in section three of this book.

He also said that he feels it is his duty to help other veterans who are going through the same experiences. "Be a brother's keeper. Everybody's war is different. But one thing we have in common is we all served and we had each other's backs there, and now we need to have each other's backs here stateside."

A list of resources where veterans and their family members can receive help in dealing with PTSD is included in the back of this book and also may be found on our companion website, www.warsendwithme.com.

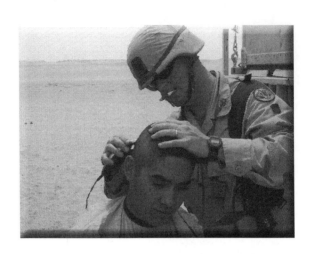

CHAPTER FOUR
A Bad Day at the VA

§

"You build on failure. You use it as a stepping stone. Close the door on the past. You don't try to forget the mistakes, but you don't dwell on it. You don't let it have any of your energy, or any of your time, or any of your space."
~ *Johnny Cash*

It was just supposed to be a simple appointment to be fitted for a new hearing aid. But like so many other things that start out simple, it quickly turned into a situation which spiraled out of control and threatened to trigger the kind of episode Patrick fights to suppress, especially when he's out in public places.

"Most people have a 1 to 10 gauge," said Patrick. "I used to be one of those people. Now I have either a 1 or a 10, and nothing in between."

While he can feel it happening, rarely can he suppress or even control it.

On November 13, 2014, Patrick arrived at the Veterans Administration Center in Iowa City, IA for an appointment for his new hearing aids – devices he has required since sustaining his injuries in Iraq. The center is more than an hour from Patrick's home, requiring that he arrange for the day off from work in order to attend appointments. When he attempted to check in for his appointment, the receptionist told him there was no record of him having an appointment for that day. She refused to help him further other than to reschedule him — for mid-December.

Trying his best to stay composed, Patrick knew he was headed for a 10. He reached out to a friend via text to talk him off the ledge. Sensing his state of mind, Patrick's friend then reached out to the patient advocate office at the VA, and an advocate was sent to help him.

It's not the first time Patrick's PTSD has reared its ugly head in a very public fashion.

One of the worst incidents he has ever had in public happened shortly after he was officially diagnosed with PTSD. He was pulling into a gas station parking lot, only to discover all of the spaces were full except for one. He chose not to park in the only open space because to do so would have resulted in his vehicle blocking another. So he decided to take a lap in the hopes that a space would eventually open up, and it did. However, when he pulled in to the newly-open space, another driver advised him in a not-so-polite manner that he should park elsewhere.

"I instantly went to a 10," said Patrick. "I approached him and threatened to beat the hell out of him right there. That is just not me, not my style to behave that way, but I was so agitated I couldn't control myself."

Thankfully, he managed to get his emotions in check. But the experience was enough to scare him. "This is the side of myself that really scares me because I go from 1 to 10 and I can't control it. I'm just embarrassed and ashamed afterward."

There have been other incidents that Patrick recalls over the last decade, each leaving him embarrassed and irritated at his inability to control his actions. One such incident occurred at work, when a coworker interrupted him when he was having a heated discussion with someone else. "I got extremely upset and verbally abusive and pretty much put him in his place. I felt really bad about it later."

Patrick has never gotten physically aggressive with anyone, something he considers a small miracle given his inability to manage his temper.

A Veterans Administration psychiatrist Patrick worked with after he was first diagnosed suggested that Patrick needed to eliminate the stressors that can cause him to go to 10. Stressors, also known as triggers, can consist of sights, sounds, smells and even feelings that bring back memories of the trauma that originally caused the PTSD. It was advice that may have sounded good on paper but was impractical when it came to applying it to real life.

"What aren't my triggers?" Patrick said. "It would seem that I have a lot of them, because it seems like I have at least one event a day that can send me to a 10."

Because he has had difficulty determining exactly what can send him to that raging 10, Patrick has spent most of the last 10 years as a bit of a recluse. He manages to go to work, but he avoids other social situations as much as possible. "I'm fearful that I'll lose my job because of my issues," Patrick said. "I'm fearful that I'll lose my family because of my issues."

Donna Strobel, who has been married to Patrick for more than two decades, said it has been hard watching the man she fell in love with in high school go through such a dramatic personality change. "Immediately, he was a different person, and unfortunately, things got worse," she said of when Patrick first returned from Iraq. "I thought he was going to get better, but unfortunately, things just got worse."

Donna said her husband was short-tempered and had no patience, which was not like the man she knew before he went to Iraq. She felt herself moving into the role of family negotiator more and more — a role she was uncomfortable with but realized was necessary if she hoped to help navigate her family through Pat's struggles with PTSD. It's a role that, over the last decade, hasn't changed. "Still to this day, I have to step in and be the family mediator."

Being the family mediator isn't the only new role Donna has taken on since Pat's PTSD diagnosis. She also has become the family problem-solver and family manager. "I have to be," she said. "Pat thinks things are worse than they are so now, unless it's life or death, I do most of the family management on my own. It's just not worth it to get him involved."

Donna also is the all-around peacemaker in situations with perfect strangers. She can recount several times that Pat has lost his cool in public and over the smallest things. She recalled a time at the DMV when Pat went off on a lady over something so trivial it scared Donna. "If I can diffuse a situation before it goes haywire, I will, but it doesn't always happen in every instance. Now, if he's going to be out, I have to be with him to distract him so his behavior doesn't escalate."

Patrick has missed out on a lot in the last decade, including a recent trip he was supposed to take to California because he was too anxious to fly. When he and his family first moved to Iowa from the Chicago, Ill. area, Patrick never went anywhere without a weapon. "For about eight or nine years, I carried a weapon on the rare events we went out," he said. "I missed a lot of my kids' events. If I did go, we would have to plan well in advance so that I could try to prepare myself mentally to go. Sometimes I would go to places, and just hang out by the door."

Even when he prepares himself, there is always the possibility that something he had not anticipated will trigger his PTSD. Bent over telephone poles, or rundown buildings, will immediately transport him back to the streets of Iraq and Afghanistan. "Anything that has any destruction to it, it takes me right back, because that's all I ever saw over there was destruction. Sometimes, there's just no advance warning."

It is not uncommon for those with PTSD to find themselves being triggered by every day, normal events and activities that others around them are able to complete without issue, or even enjoy. For veterans like Patrick – who were involved or injured in attacks on their convoys during active deployment – operating a motor vehicle once back home may trigger anxiety and anger. "It used to really bother me," Patrick said. "Back in 2004, I used to get flashbacks when I'd try to drive. I don't get them anymore, though."

Watching an action movie, especially one that involves military scenes or other violence of a similar nature, can be intolerable for some veterans with PTSD. Patrick hasn't tried to watch a movie in over a decade and said that movies like Restrepo and other war-time documentaries are too personal for him and he chooses not to watch them. "I tried to watch a documentary on PTSD once and couldn't get through it," he said.

Joe Madrid said it has been a long journey with his PTSD, and part of the process of dealing with it has been the acceptance that there are just some things he is no longer able to do. "My son plays pro football and I used to go to his games, but I can't do that anymore. Being around large crowds – or rowdy people who are drinking – and all the noise are just triggers for me."

Even though he knows his triggers, Madrid said he has made more than one mistake in thinking he could tolerate an outing that he logically knew he should avoid. Last year, Madrid said he decided to attend a huge outdoor concert while in California with his wife. He said he managed to do OK until the last act of the night, when it became even more crowded at the venue with people packing it in to see the final act. "People kept getting closer and closer to me, and I just lost it. My wife was able to get me out of there and calmed down, but it was a mistake I should never have made."

Angel Mojica, who we met in an earlier chapter, said large crowds are always a trigger for his PTSD. "I was always in a constant alert mode and I wasn't a big fan of going to the mall or large concerts." Noises by themselves didn't seem to bother him, but the smell of something burning – especially the smell of burning trash – consistently set him off because it reminded him of being in the streets of Iraq.

While it is important to make sure you do not become socially isolated when dealing with PTSD, it also is necessary to know which social situations may actually trigger your PTSD so that they can be avoided. The National Center for PTSD lists a number of situations which can trigger PTSD symptoms in veterans with the condition, and recommends veterans who are dealing with PTSD might wish to avoid the following activities:

• 	Closely following media coverage of war or military operations similar to those which caused their PTSD;
• 	Exposure to violent or disturbing images from television shows or movies; and
• 	Gatherings for veterans which may include emotional components (Veterans' Day services, July 4th celebrations).

The center also said avoidance of things that remind combat veterans of the events which led to their PTSD is normal and that it is best to let the veteran decide whether an event or situation is something they will be able to reasonably handle, or if they should avoid.

Madrid said he does not want to sound discouraging, but that, "There is no magic cure. There are some things I will just never forget, because it's sad the things people will do to each other. Iraq took such a toll on me." Madrid said with the proper therapy, veterans can learn to cope and to continue on with life but must accept that there are just some things they might not be able to do anymore. "It can be frustrating and disappointing, but there are just some things I can't do anymore, and I accept that."

Section II
America is at the Mall

****

"Often it isn't the initiating trauma that creates seemingly in-surmountable pain, but the lack of support thereafter."

~S. Kelley Harrell, Author
Gift of the Dreamtime: Awakening to the Divinity of Trauma

****

CHAPTER FIVE
The Homefront Battle

§

*"We must learn to regard people less in the light of what
they do or omit to do, and more in the light of what they suffer."*
~Dietrich Bonhoeffer

Perhaps the only thing worse than being afflicted with PTSD is coming home to find that those around you are blissfully unaware of the pain you live with every day. It's not that most people have never heard of PTSD; rather, it's that many of them are unable to fully grasp how it affects the complete person – heart, body, mind and soul. Only those who have endured the kind of trauma that often results in PTSD can truly relate.

"For people who have never been in combat, it's hard to understand what it is like," said Dr. Sudip Bose, a practicing emergency room physician, motivational speaker and combat veteran. "Education is the best way to spread awareness and acceptance."

Dr. Bose has made it his mission to gain understanding and acceptance of PTSD, as both are crucial components to helping the nearly 30 percent of veterans who are returning from war with PTSD. As a combat veteran with medical training, he offers a unique perspective on dealing with the after effects of combat trauma.

His family moved to the United States from Calcutta, India in the

1960s. Wanting the full American experience, Dr. Bose said he enlisted in the U.S. Army at age 21. Dr. Bose, like so many other American men and women, volunteered to serve in an active combat zone when the U.S. entered Iraq following the Sept. 11 terrorist attacks. "It was an honor and a privilege taking care of those soldiers over there," he said.

He knows firsthand what the stress of combat can do to our soldiers. Dr. Bose served for nearly 15 months as a physician on the front lines in Iraq with the U.S. Army First Cavalry Division. His was one of the longest physician tours during active combat since World War II.

In early 2004, he rushed to the aid of survivors who were injured during a celebration of an Iraqi holiday that ended when three suicide bombers detonated the devices strapped to their chests. The only physician in a sea of people with life-threatening injuries, Dr. Bose became overwhelmed, realizing he couldn't possibly treat everyone who needed it by himself. So he sought the assistance of the medics on his team – medics who previously had been trained by Dr. Bose to respond in a combat-trauma situation such as the one they currently faced. It was their quick response that helped to save many lives that day.

In addition to his combat field service, Dr. Bose also was the physician who treated Saddam Hussein following his capture in December 2003.

Dr. Bose received the Bronze Star for his meritorious service in Iraq – the first Indian American to do so.

Following his tour of duty, Dr. Bose found himself thrust into the spotlight and into the role of public speaker, which was not something he had planned. "So, I decided to use it to my advantage," he said. "I'm trying to have the multiplier effect. I asked myself how I can take my experience and use it to help others. I want to make a bigger impact."

The result of his efforts to use his notoriety for good is *The Battle Continues*, a nonprofit organization designed to promote a better understanding of the healthcare issues affecting the men and women who have dedicated their lives to defending and serving their country. Every cent donated to the foundation – including Dr. Bose's fees for appearing as a motivational or guest speaker at functions and events – goes toward providing medical treatments and other services to veterans in need of assistance.

One of the things Dr. Bose has been most vocal about is PTSD. While Dr. Bose does not have PTSD himself, he has experienced the kind of combat situations that easily can cause veterans to develop PTSD. "I think the main reason I didn't (develop PTSD) is because I had an unfair advantage over other veterans," he said. "As a doctor, I had seen a lot of medical carnage and death, so I think I was better prepared than some of the 18- or 19-year-olds who went there."

Dr. Bose said he feels fortunate not to have developed PTSD and wants to improve veterans' access to care when they are dealing with PTSD. He also wants to increase awareness among the general population about how PTSD manifests itself and what can be done to help those who are fighting it every day. One of the educational tools he uses is a lecture series that takes an audience through a virtual combat experience. While it's not the same as being physically present in a combat zone, it provides an effective simulation and helps an audience to understand why soldiers come back from war with feelings of guilt, anxiety and anger.

"I truly believe that education is the key to ending the stigma associated with PTSD," Dr. Bose said. "People are seeing the physical wounds of our soldiers, but there are a lot of mental abrasions that can't be seen. There is no EKG, no CAT scan that can show them. These injuries are invisible."

That stigma is something with which Patrick is all too familiar. "People don't really get the seriousness of it," he said. "I get tired of trying to explain to people why I react the way I do. I really hate it when people startle me and then laugh at my reaction because they just do not get it."

Patrick recounted an incident where a coworker thought it was funny to see his reaction when startled and would go out of his way to see if he could rattle Patrick, so he could get a good laugh out of it. "I try to choke it back when it happens, but if I tell someone why I am easily startled, and they do it again after that, then I get angry."

He's never gotten physically aggressive with anyone when his PTSD is triggered, but he has been somewhat verbally abusive to others. When that happens, he then gets angry with himself for losing control. Patrick recalled a recent time at work when he was having a heated discussion and a coworker interrupted him. The interruption caused him to become extremely upset and verbally abusive to the coworker who had caused the interruption. "I pretty much put him in his place, and then I felt really bad about it later."

Because he has no warning before it happens, and because people are not always sympathetic to his needs when he explains them, Patrick has tried to be proactive in preventing the kind of disturbances that typically trigger his PTSD. One of the things he has done at work to prevent outbursts is to use a mirror on his desk, so he can see what is directly behind him. Now, if someone approaches his desk, he is able to see them coming, which eliminates that element of surprise and greatly reduces his chances of being startled.

Patrick also is more forgiving of strangers who accidentally trigger his PTSD than he is of his own family members. "I get really mad at my family, because I think they should know how this works by now and should try not to get upset if I act out," he said. "But when they don't, and they get upset by my behavior, then I get more upset and it just amplifies it."

Josh Strobel said it was challenging, at times, to watch his dad going through it, knowing there wasn't really anything he could do to help him except try to be understanding and give him either the space – or the support – needed. "It's been hard, but we've worked through it. We're a family, and always will be a family, no matter what."

Nancy Lambert said it has been hard watching her son deal with PTSD for over a decade, and it doesn't get any easier just because they have been on the front lines with him for so long. Lambert gives a lot of credit to Patrick's wife, Donna, for sticking with him. "I love her for being such a strong woman," she said.

Donna Strobel said it has been difficult, at times, to look at Patrick and see him as the same man she married over two decades ago. The PTSD has changed his personality so much that some days, she doesn't recognize him. "He's not the same person that I once knew," she said. "It's a struggle some days because I just get so aggravated, say I'm done and can't do this anymore . . . and then I remind myself that he's still here. He didn't die that day and I am grateful to still have him with me. It overwhelms me when I think of the demons he deals with every day. But I'm here for the long haul and he's not getting rid of me. He's my soul mate."

Janine Madrid understands the pain Donna Strobel experiences every day, because she has been through it herself. She met her husband, Joe, in the late 1970s when both were serving in the military. Madrid said she never realized how far-reaching the effects of PTSD could be on someone until she experienced it with Joe in 2005.

Like Patrick, Joe dealt with explosive anger he could neither explain nor control. He would become easily frustrated if he was unable to complete a task as quickly as he felt it should be done. And, like many veterans with PTSD, he would want to be in control of every situation and every person in order to feel like any risk to his own well being had been eliminated. When out in public, Joe would scan his surroundings and then choose where to position himself so that he could best control the situation. "I always had to deal with the loss of control. The minute he couldn't control a situation, it would set him off."

Madrid said she tolerated a lot because she loved her husband and desperately wanted him to be the man he was before his deployment to the Middle East. But the day he threatened to kill a co-worker was the day she decided it was time to put some distance between herself and her husband. "I'm not proud to say it, but I couldn't deal with it anymore. I feared what he might do."

The Madrids remained separated until Joe acknowledged and then sought treatment for his PTSD. Once he got the help that he needed, Madrid returned home to her husband. While he still has rough days, Joe's ability to handle his PTSD has improved significantly. When asked if she'd ever consider leaving again, Madrid said for her, it is not an option. "For me not to stay; I'd be giving up on him – and I don't want to give up on him, because he's a good man."

While it is incredibly difficult for family members – who are on the front lines of their loved one's battle with PTSD daily – to cope, there are things that can be done to help a person with PTSD.

First and foremost, **never say to the person that you know how they feel.** While most of us have been taught that those words are a sign of empathy and can provide comfort to someone in pain, that rule does not apply when talking with someone with PTSD. Those words will mostly likely further upset the veteran who has experienced far worse things than any of us will ever have to endure in our lifetimes. The only person who should ever make a statement like that to a veteran with PTSD is another veteran who also is dealing with PTSD, or who has been in a combat situation themselves and understands how that experience can change a person.

Don't push someone with PTSD into talking if they aren't

able to do so. Let them share on their own time and in their own way. When they do talk – no matter how difficult it is to hear what they may be saying – be an active listener. The best response you can offer is to tell them that you are there for them and will listen when they are ready to share.

Madrid shared the first time her husband ever told her what he was thinking when he was having an anxiety attack from the PTSD: "The first time he ever told me about when he was having a moment was when we were sitting and drinking a glass of wine together. He just stared at his wine, and told me that it reminded him of blood, and then he started telling me about how he was a bad person because he killed people. Nobody ever prepares you to hear this from your husband."

Veterans who are having difficulty expressing their feelings by talking about them should be encouraged to write about them. Many therapists who treat PTSD patients will encourage them to put their thoughts on paper. It can be as elaborate as keeping a daily journal about their combat experiences, PTSD triggers and other difficulties they have experienced since returning from active duty, to something as simple as writing down an experience, crumpling up the paper it is written on and then throwing it away. Some veterans, like Patrick, have chosen to put their experiences into a book in an attempt to not only help themselves, but also to help other veterans who are dealing with PTSD.

Deep breathing exercises can help if you sense that your loved one has encountered a PTSD trigger. Get them to a quiet place where they can focus on breathing and, if necessary, have a more private setting if they are unable to cope and have a breakdown. One of the only things worse than dealing with a PTSD anxiety attack or outburst of anger is doing so in a very public forum. "I don't want people to see me that way," said Patrick. "It only increases my anxiety or my anger if I know it's happening and I can't control it, and then people are staring at me while it's happening."

Avoid drugs and alcohol. Unfortunately, many veterans turn to drugs and alcohol to deal with PTSD in an attempt to dull the pain. Having PTSD increases a veteran's chance to develop a drug or alcohol abuse problem. Statistics from the U.S. Department of Veterans Affairs indicate that more than two out of every 10 veterans with PTSD also develop Substance Abuse Disorder (SUD). The department also noted that war veterans with PTSD who already had alcohol control issues are more likely to become binge drinkers. If a friend or loved one with PTSD is turning to drugs and alcohol in an attempt to control their PTSD, please encourage them to seek out a treatment program that addresses both PTSD and SUD at the same time.

Encourage the veteran to seek therapy or counseling. Therapy can consist of one-on-one sessions with a psychologist or counselor, or group therapy situations where other veterans dealing with PTSD can work through it together. Hearing that they are not alone and sharing their story with other veterans who understand can be very beneficial to veterans with PTSD. Veterans are not the only ones who may benefit from counseling. Family members also are encouraged to seek counseling to help them cope with their loved one's PTSD. For married couples, joint marriage counseling with a therapist who is trained in PTSD therapy is ideal in helping both the spouse with PTSD and the spouse helping them to cope with it. Family therapy may be necessary when young children are involved. In addition to counseling, there are other treatments for veterans with PTSD that can help, which will be discussed in depth later in this book.

Of all the things friends and family members can do for their loved one with PTSD, the most important is to let them know that **having PTSD does not make them less of a person in your eyes.** Being able to admit they are struggling, and seeking professional help to deal with the PTSD, makes them strong, not weak. "It's important for them to know they're not alone," said Madrid.

CHAPTER SIX
The Brain-Body Connection
§

"A mental stain can neither be blotted out by the passage of time nor washed away by any waters."
~*Cicero*

The effects of PTSD on the brain are well documented. Areas of the brain involved in the stress response that is trigged by PTSD include the amygdala, hippocampus and prefrontal cortex.

According to a study conducted by J. Douglas Bremner, M.D., traumatic stress is associated with permanent changes to these areas of the brain. The study states that "patients with PTSD show increased cortisol and norepinephrine responses to stress." Bremner's findings suggest that the brain of a person with PTSD perceives every situation as a threat, placing the body in a constant state of "fight or flight."

Also known as the acute stress response, fight or flight first was discovered by Dr. Walter B. Cannon in 1915. Dr. Cannon studied at Harvard University and went on to become a teacher in the Department of Physiology. His fascination with the physical reactions of his laboratory animals while under stress led to the discovery, which prompted him to further study all of the body's physiological reactions to stress.

Fight or flight is an automatic response to stressful – and often physically dangerous – situations. A sort of auto pilot defense mechanism, it triggers the brain to keep the body safe by preparing it for action, which can include fighting or fleeing from the situation. The brain accomplishes this automatic task by activating the body's sympathetic nervous system, which is designed to stimulate the body and mobilize its energy resources.

The release of adrenaline and norepinephrine from the medulla is triggered by acetylcholine from the preganglionic sympathetic nerves. Among the physiological changes in the body when it launches into fight or flight mode include accelerated heart rate, increased blood flow to the muscles, increased lung capacity and the release of adrenaline and other hormones.

In a brain that is functioning normally, the fight or flight response is activated only in a true life-threatening situation; however, in someone with PTSD, even the misperception of a threat can launch the body into full-blown acute stress response. Individuals who are unable to turn off the stress response can become overweight due to the buildup of fatty tissue caused by increased cortisol levels in the body. The increased cortisol levels also damage blood vessels and arteries, which raises blood pressure and the risk of having a heart attack or stroke.

In addition to the physical health issues a prolonged state of fight or flight can cause, it also takes a toll on the brain itself.

Daniela Kaufer, a UC Berkeley associate professor of integrative biology, conducted a series of experiments that revealed chronic stress and elevated cortisol levels – such as the kind produced by PTSD – generate overproduction of myelin-producing cells and fewer neurons. Her findings were published in the February 11, 2014 issue of Molecular Psychiatry.

The brain consists of both gray matter and white matter, each with its own purpose. Gray matter is responsible for the brain's higher functioning, which includes thinking, processing and making decisions. White matter consists of axons, which are the network of fibers interconnecting neurons and creating a communications network between the gray and white matter regions of the brain.

Kaufer's research found that prolonged fight or flight responses changed how the hippocampus functions and causes too much white matter to form in some areas of the brain. This over-growth of white matter dramatically slows the brain's ability to communicate with itself and the body by decreasing the number of stem cells that are able to mature into neurons. With fewer mature neurons, the individual becomes more susceptible to other mental disorders in the future, including memory loss.

Bremner's and Kaufer's research is among the many exploring the effects of PTSD on both the brain and the body.

Several studies have suggested the length of deployment has a direct effect on whether a veteran will develop PTSD. Dr. Roger Brooke, Director of Military Services at Duquesne University, said he agrees with those theories.

"Studies have shown deployments longer than six months almost always increase the chances of developing PTSD," Dr. Brooke said. According to the RAND Corporation – a nonprofit institution that uses research and analysis to help improve policy and decision-making – the cumulative amount of time a soldier has spent deployed has increased by 28 percent since 2008. The information was published as part of RAND's Measuring Army Deployments to Iraq and Afghanistan report, compiled by Dave Baiocchi.

According to the report, RAND was asked by the Vice Chief of Staff of the U.S. Army to assess the demands being placed on the Army specifically by deployments to Operation Iraqi Freedom and Operation Enduring Freedom in Afghanistan. Some of the key findings of the report include:

• Roughly 73 percent of active-component soldiers had deployed to Iraq, Afghanistan or both by 2011, which was up from 67 percent in 2008;

• The 27 percent of soldiers who had not yet deployed were found to be current recruits, those who were forward-stationed in other overseas locations or had contributed to the operations in Iraq and/or Afghanistan through direct support while stationed stateside; and

• The Army's ability to deploy additional active-component soldiers was impossible without also lengthening the deployments or shortening the time between deployments for each soldier, both of which would increase the burden on those who already had served a previous deployment.

The report also indicates that the Army provided 54 percent – or four in seven of the total deployments among all Armed Forces – to operations in Iraq and Afghanistan. In comparison, the Navy supplied 17 percent of its forces, the Air Force offered 15 percent and the Marine Corps accounted for 14 percent. "The Army has provided over 1.5 million troop-years to operations in Iraq and Afghanistan," the report states. Data also concluded that 38,000 of the Army's soldiers had spent at least 12 months of their time in the Army deployed, while 40,500 spent 13 months deployed and 9,800 had accumulated 14 months or more of deployed time.

"Since 2008, the cumulative amount of time that a soldier has spent deployed has increased by an average of 28 percent," the report states. "Of particular note are the 136,000 AC soldiers working on their second year of cumulative deployment time and an additional 136,000 AC soldiers working on their third year or longer of cumulative deployment time."

Dr. Brooke said it is not just the length and number of deployments combat veterans are being subjected to, which increases their chances of developing PTSD. It also is the brutality and intensity of the situations being experienced during the repeat deployments that further impacts veterans. "My own son served in Iraq and he told me there were times that he'd get shot at an average of 30 times per night. He once went through an entire month of intense fighting that left him with no time to change his clothes or anything else. The scale is just incredible and it's brutal."

One of the tactics the military has employed to help prepare combat soldiers for these stress-under-fire situations is called resiliency training. Some branches of the military refer to the technique as "Mindfulness," in which soldiers learn how to keep their brain attentive and in the moment without issuing judgment of the situation. The idea behind the technique is that by psychologically preparing members of the military to face dangerous, high-performance and high-stress situations while in combat, they will be less plagued by mental-health issues when they return from deployment.

The STRONG Project (Schofield Barracks Training and Research on Neurobehavioral Growth), conducted by neuroscientist Dr. Amishi Jha, began in April 2010 and is still active. Dr. Jha and her team at the University of Miami were awarded a $1.72 million grant to manage the project, which is designed to track the impact of pre-deployment resilience training during the course of the deployment cycle. The project uses computer-based experiments and brainwave recording to determine whether resilience training improves the ways a brain pays attention, is aware of immediate surroundings and manages and recovers from stress. Providing soldiers with a sort of mental armor is the intended goal of resilience training.

Three groups of military service members were studied as part of the STRONG Project. The groups consisted of 75 soldiers who were stationed at Schofield Barracks in Hawaii who were eight to 10 months away from a deployment to Afghanistan. Of the three groups, two received Mindfulness training and one did not. One of the two groups to receive Mindfulness training received a specific kind called Mindfulness-based Mind Fitness Training (MMFT), which emphasizes engagement during class meetings. The other group received Mindfulness training that was comprised of didactic information and discussions revolving around resilience and stress. While the methods were different, both groups reported more awareness of their attention, which was interpreted to mean the MMFT was effective. Dr. Jha's report suggests that just 24 hours of Mindfulness training for service members leads to improvements in mood and cognitive function. Dr. Jha published her complete findings in "Minds 'At Attention': Mindfulness Training Curbs Attentional Lapses in Military Cohorts. The report can be found online at journals.plos.org.

While Dr. Jha's findings seem promising, not everyone shares in her enthusiasm for its success. Dr. Brooke said he believes the training – while well-intentioned – can have dreaded unintended consequences. Soldiers who undergo resilience training, yet still develop PTSD post combat, may be harder on themselves than their counterparts who did not receive the pre-deployment training and developed PTSD. "I believe that giving them clichés might actually produce more instances of PTSD because they'll feel like failures and ashamed if (resilience training) doesn't work."

Dr. Brooke isn't the only psychology professional who believes the method may be overrated.

Roy Eidelson, Ph.D., and co-author Stephen Soldz published a piece in June 2012 that states the military's resilience training program isn't as effective as the military has claimed. In the article titled The Army's Flawed Resilience-Training Study: A Call for Retraction, Eidelson states there is little evidence to suggest this kind of training works. "Since its inception, CSF has been the target of numerous criticisms from psychologists and others . . . concerns raised by critics span a wide range of significant issues," Eidelson writes. "The research evaluating the program is of questionable quality and it does not support the strong claims being made about CSF's effectiveness."

Eidelson critiques several parts of the report but emphasizes that the third section outlining the Master Resilience Trainer component is the most flawed. The MRT component includes an intensive 10-day training course for military leaders, who are then placed in charge of units and required to share those skills and strategies with soldiers that are supposed to help with handling the physical and psychological challenges of military life, including combat operations.

He detailed several areas of weakness in the methods used by the military to determine the effectiveness of the component:
• The researchers' failure to measure the important outcomes of PTSD, depression or other psychological disorders;
• A flawed research design that fails to account for important confounding variables;
• Numerous problems with the method of data analysis; and
• The failure on the part of researchers to acknowledge plausible risks of harm from the process.

"Based on our careful analysis of Report #3, we believe that the claims of CSF proponents regarding the program's effectiveness are vastly inflated," Eidelson writes. "We therefore call upon the Army to retract this report or, at a minimum, issue an unambiguous and widely disseminated statement acknowledging that the report is seriously flawed and that, as a result, the verdict is still out on whether CSF actually works."

Eidelson goes on to state in his report that the psychological health of the nation's military members is a top priority, and that the alarming rates of PTSD, suicide and other behavioral and emotional difficulties which affect our troops, must be addressed. "But it is simply wrong at this time to present CSF as part of a solution," he writes, "because to date, there is no solid empirical evidence demonstrating that the program accomplishes any of these lofty goals."

CHAPTER SEVEN
Take it Like a Man: PTSD and Gender

§

"Even in times of trauma, we try to maintain a sense of normality until we no longer can. That, my friends, is called surviving. Not healing. We never become whole again . . . we are survivors. If you are here today . . . you are a survivor. But those of us who have made it through hell and are still standing? We bear a different name: warriors."
~Lori Goodwin, Veteran and Author

In January 2013, the formal process to open combat jobs to women began. Three years later, Defense Secretary Ash Carter announced that women serving in all branches of the U.S. military would now be permitted to serve in combat posts.

In his official announcement, Carter stated that women would be "allowed to drive tanks, fire mortars and lead infantry soldiers into combat . . . they'll be able to serve as Army Rangers and Green Berets, Navy SEALs, Marine Corps infantry, Air Force parajumpers and everything else that was previously open only to men."

While some lauded the change, others expressed concerns, including fears over whether women would be able to handle the intense physical and emotional demands of soldiers serving on the front lines. Of particular concern was the increased possibility of women coming home from war with PTSD.

Women with PTSD, however, are not a new phenomenon, and certainly not one exclusively associated with their new roles on the front lines. Prior to women being able to serve in active combat situations, they still were being subjected to the kinds of trauma that can result in PTSD. In addition to combat operations, women can develop PTSD due to military sexual trauma, or the stress associated with worry about their children or other family members during deployment.

According to the U.S. Department of Veterans Affairs, 20 percent of women who have served tours in Iraq and Afghanistan have been diagnosed with PTSD. It's not the first time women have developed PTSD following active duty. The National Vietnam Veterans Readjustment Study, which included 1,632 female Vietnam veterans, revealed that 27 percent of women who served suffered from PTSD at some point in time following active duty.

The readjustment study is not the only one the VA has conducted concerning PTSD and gender. In October 2012, the Journal of Psychiatric Research published a study conducted by Dr. Sabra Inslicht, a staff psychologist at the San Francisco VA Medical Center and assistant professor of psychiatry at the University of California. The study closely examined the differences between how men and women develop fear and what role it may play in which sex is more susceptible to PTSD.

Eighteen men and 13 women who had developed PTSD due to combat, sexual assault, physical assault or accidents were included in the study. The participants were conditioned to expect to receive an electrical stimulus in association with certain images being flashed on a screen. The electrical shocks were at a level that was considered annoying but not painful for participants. Researchers measured electrical conductance in the participants' skin to track moisture changes associated with the presentation of the images. The moisture changes were a reflection of emotional response, including fear.

What Dr. Inslicht found was that women are at greater risk of developing PTSD due to a heightened fear response. While learning fear can be an important tool for survival, the inability to turn it off in safe situations causes wear and tear on the mind and the body which can result in the development of PTSD.

"Understanding possible gender differences more precisely could put us in a position to develop much more effective, focused therapies for PTSD," the report concluded.

Kate Dahlstedt, M.A., Program Director and Co-Founder of Soldier's Heart, has worked with both male and female veterans and their families for nearly three decades. Dahlstedt and her husband, Dr. Edward Tick, created the Soldier's Heart Model, which is used to help veterans and their families struggling with PTSD and the reintroduction back into civilian life. We talk more about this model in Chapter 11 of this book.

Dahlstedt said she is not surprised women are more susceptible to developing PTSD, nor is she shocked they have been developing it long before they were permitted to serve during combat on the front lines. "Women, while not in direct combat missions, are still at war," she said. "War is everywhere around them. They are not tucked away somewhere safe."

Women serving on medical teams, on infantry teams and even those responsible for conducting pat downs or other interactions with female residents in war zones are all exposed to the kind of stimuli that can contribute to developing PTSD. Women also are more likely to be sexually assaulted – even in a war zone – than their male counterparts. "Sexual harassment and assault is an added PTSD component for female vets," she said. "Over half of all women veterans who come to us have been harassed or assaulted."

A 2011 article published in Research in Nursing and Health titled "More Than Military Sexual Trauma: Interpersonal Violence, PTSD, and Mental Health in Women Veterans"(Kelly, Skelton, Patel, Bradley) indicated that military sexual trauma was a major contributing factor in women veterans developing PTSD. According to the article, one in every four female veterans polled by the Veterans Administration reported experiencing sexual trauma while serving on active duty.

When combined with other combat-related trauma – including both physical and psychological traumatic events such as receiving enemy fire or being ambushed by hostile forces while outside of the base camp – military sexual trauma can create the perfect storm for female veterans to develop PTSD.

A separate article, titled "Military Sexual Trauma Among U.S. Female Veterans," (Irene Williams and Kunsook Bernstein) offers further supporting evidence that women are more susceptible to developing PTSD when military sexual assault is factored into the equation. A 2003 study commissioned by the U.S. Department of Defense (DOD) placed the number of incidents of women veterans experiencing sexual assault during active duty at 3 percent as compared with 1 percent of their male counterparts. The DOD report defines sexual assault as rape, forcible sodomy and indecent assault.

Another factor in female veterans developing PTSD more frequently than men is their natural tendency to be nurturers, which can be counter to what is expected of a soldier in a war zone, said Dahlstedt. "Women are told they can't express compassion, which is harder for them than men because of how we're raised and the way women are seen in society."

A study by Roberto Mercadillo of the National Autonomous University of Mexico, titled "Perception of Suffering and Compassion Experience: Brain Gender Disparities," compared men and women's brain activation while they were experiencing compassion.

Male and female participants in Mercadillo's study were asked to lie in a Functional Magnetic Resonance Imaging (fMRI) machine while they were experiencing the feeling of compassion. An fMRI machine uses MRI technology to measure brain activity associated with blood flow. Male and female participants were exposed to the same images designed to trigger compassion while being monitored by the fMRI.

While both male and female participants reported feeling the same level of compassion while viewing the images intended to evoke the emotion, Mercadillo discovered that the regions of the brain activated in the male participants differed from the females. Although his findings do not indicate that women experience compassion more than men, it does suggest that men and women differ in how they experience and express compassion.

Walking a Mile in Her Combat Boots

Eva Foster, like so many others, enlisted in the U.S. Army following the events of the September 11, 2001 terrorist attack on New York, Pennsylvania and Washington, D.C. She was commissioned in August of 2002 and went on to complete Intelligence Officer training. She deployed to Iraq in 2004.

When Foster talks about her PTSD – and the experience in Iraq that led up to the development of it – she uses language that easily can be mistaken for that of a soldier reciting a mission order. "My therapist told me I do that because it's my way of being able to talk about it without it affecting me."

Foster is not alone in her rote dictation of the events leading up to her development of PTSD. It is a common coping mechanism for many members of the military who are struggling to overcome the situation and circumstances which have caused them so much mental anguish. For Foster, that event happened on June 22, 2004 during a routine ground patrol her unit was conducting in Balad, Iraq. She was stationed with the Alpha Company, 579th Engineer Battalion. "Our task force was in charge of training the Iraqi National Guard. On that day, two of the Iraqis we were training turned their guns on us during an ambush situation."

Two of her fellow soldiers – Army 2nd Lt. Andre D. Tyson and Army Specialist Patrick R. McCaffrey Sr. – were killed in the ambush. "That is what caused my PTSD."

Foster continued to serve in Iraq until September of 2004, when she was injured during an indirect fire incident in Anaconda, Iraq. She suffered a traumatic brain injury during the attack, along with injuries to her shoulder and leg. It would be several years before Foster's friends and family members began to suspect she was dealing with more than just a traumatic brain injury from her time in Iraq.

In 2007, Foster went on tour in Naples, Italy. It was following her Naples tour that her friends and family began to notice that she seemed uncomfortable in public places, had an increasingly uncontrollable temper and was set off by certain noises. "I didn't recognize it for what it was, but my Aunt Fran recognized it was PTSD. When she told me, I just blew it off." Looking back, Foster says she believes it was the conditions in Naples – conditions she described as dirty and crime-ridden – that triggered memories of another place she had served that was very similar: Iraq.

Following her tour in Naples, Foster returned to Arizona while her husband was serving an active deployment in Iraq. It wasn't until 2014, however, that she began to accept that something besides the traumatic brain injury was affecting her behavior. "If I was out, I'd want to sit with my back to the wall. I didn't want to leave the house unless it was absolutely necessary."

But it wasn't until the death of her father – and a strange, cold sensation she had after praying for her fallen friends to come "escort" her dad to Heaven – that she plunged headlong into her PTSD and was no longer able to ignore it. "After that, the nightmares came back. My situational awareness was heightened again. The final straw was when I hurt someone at work."

In December of 2014, Foster lost her temper during an intake procedure for a prisoner re-entry. The prisoner tried to get physical with her, and she reacted by getting physical back. "I used techniques on him that I learned to subdue terrorists in war time, which was not something I was supposed to do in this situation. I completely overreacted and injured him." Foster was immediately sent to the Veterans Administration hospital for evaluation. The clinician at the VA concluded she had severe PTSD and required immediate treatment. "When she told me that I had pretty severe PTSD. I told her no, I didn't."

It wasn't until she and her husband were in a crowded pizza shop with their children that she finally realized that she was, indeed, dealing with PTSD. "I got really overwhelmed by the crowd and the noise and I did something that I wouldn't normally do – I completely freaked out on my husband. Thankfully, he took a step back and realized that I was having a panic attack, and so did I. And that was when I decided to go back to the VA." Foster was prescribed medication for her PTSD, but admits that she rarely takes it.

Dealing with her PTSD has been complicated by a number of factors, including the fact that she is a woman. Foster said she is angry at the double standard that is shown toward women who are injured in service to their country. "My biggest frustration with how all of this was handled was I was told that women don't get hurt in combat. The very first time I was told that was while I was being Medevac'd from Iraq."

Foster said it is about time the VA – and the general public – realizes that women not only serve in active combat, they suffer serious and irreversible injuries doing so. "There are women amputees. They flew missions and were outside the wire, too. They act like women never saw combat . . . were never in the thick of things. That needs to change."

Presentation of Symptoms and Treatment Options

Identifying PTSD in both men and women can be challenging, as it presents in different ways depending on gender.

According to the National Center for PTSD, some symptoms of PTSD are more common in women than in men. Women with PTSD are more likely than men to startle easily, have difficulty feeling emotions and avoid situations that remind them of the trauma that caused their PTSD. They also are more likely to suffer from depression.

In men, PTSD often presents as anger, paranoia, insomnia and difficulty concentrating. More than half of men with PTSD also abuse drugs and alcohol.

While PTSD can be difficult to diagnose, research shows that it often goes undiagnosed in women more frequently than in men.

PTSD in women also tends to be misdiagnosed as another disorder or condition, including borderline personality disorder and even depression.

The only advantage women with PTSD have over their male counterparts is that they are more likely to seek help. Although Foster has been actively treating her PTSD, she said she feels like she is still stuck in the stages of grief, guilt and anger. "I like to tell people that my PTSD is like the dementors in the Harry Potter books. In the books, they are the characters who feed on human happiness. My PTSD is like the dementors in that it sucks all my happiness away."

The Veterans Administration has made it easier for women veterans to seek assistance through the establishment of a Women Veterans hotline. The hotline may be called to receive and respond to questions from women veterans, their family members and caregivers. Available VA services and resources also may be obtained by calling the hotline. The toll-free number for the hotline is 855-829-6636. Women veterans who are in crisis are encouraged to call the main Veterans Crisis Hotline at 800-273-8255. Online assistance is available through the Confidential Veterans Chat, which can be accessed at www.veteranscrisisline.net.

There are a variety of other resources designed specifically for women veterans with PTSD or other trauma-related issues. They include:
•   Grace After Fire – this nonprofit organization focuses on providing support and assistance to women veterans who are returning from active duty so they can re-engage into civilian life as mothers, wives and daughters. More information is available at

www.graceafterfire.org.

• She S.E.R.V.E.D. Inc. – this service-driven, charitable organization was developed to Support, Enhance and Restore Veterans Every Day. It caters exclusively to women veterans and provides assistance in transitioning from military to civilian life. More information is available at www.she-served.org.

• Women's Trauma Recovery Program – part of the National Center for PTSD at Menlo Park, Calif., this program is designed to treat women veterans with PTSD. It is open to women across the country and is a 60-day residential treatment program that strongly emphasizes interpersonal skills. For more information about this program, please call (650)-493-5000, Ext. 27166.

• Women Organizing Women Veteran Advocacy – This non-profit organization provides outreach and resource services for women veterans. Its mission is to counsel, guide, and assist women veterans in opportunities for education and training and to seek government resources to improve quality of life. Included in its many services for women veterans is access to resources for women who have experienced military sexual trauma or combat-related PTSD. Visit their website at http://veteransfamiliesunited.org.

• Women Veterans Interactive – this nonprofit organization was created to address unique, and often unrecognized, challenges facing women veterans as they transition from military to civilian life. More information about the organization is available at womenveteransinteractive.org.

CHAPTER EIGHT
Anatomy of a Nation in Denial
§

"You will find peace not by trying to escape your problems, but by con-fronting them courageously. You will find peace not in denial, but in victory."
~ J. Donald Walters

It's human nature to deny the things we cannot – or will not – accept. Denial is our brain's way of coping with a difficult situation. After all, if we just refuse to accept it, then it simply cannot be true. Mind over matter, as some people like to put it.

Being in denial about having PTSD – or acknowledging that someone you know may have it – is a dangerous way to deal with it and can exacerbate PTSD symptoms for some people.

Patrick isn't shy about expressing how he feels about those around him not always understanding or accepting what it means for him to have PTSD. "When it comes to noticing and accepting that a lot of veterans returning from recent wars are dealing with PTSD, America, quite frankly, is at the mall. People are so lost in their own little worlds and have absolutely no idea what we've had to deal with, that they just can't wrap their heads around it. So, they pretend it's not happening."

But it is happening. The VA estimates that about 11 to 20 out of every 100 veterans who served during Operations Iraqi Freedom and Enduring Freedom have developed PTSD. Roughly 12 out of every 100 Gulf War veterans have PTSD, and 30 out of every 100 Vietnam veterans have been diagnosed with the condition.

Some veterans deny they may have PTSD because of the stigma associated with the condition. For others, it's about the fear of being pulled from active duty and losing the ability to carry a firearm. Even after Patrick admitted he needed help, he would go to great lengths to hide the fact that he was being treated for PTSD. Among some of the other things he did during treatment, Patrick would show up at his appointments with the VA counselor wearing civilian clothing. "I was hoping if I dressed down, that no one would know who I was or what I was doing there."

Monteleone said any time It's About the Warrior Foundation hosts an informational session about PTSD, he and other presenters are very careful about how they address the issue as not to upset veterans to the point of leaving before they can hear the entire message. "You have to be very careful with the presentation, because most people do not want to be labeled with PTSD. For some of them, it's an age thing. The Vietnam vets will come, and they will admit they have it. The younger veterans are convinced they're too tough to need the help, so they can be a little harder to reach."

Dr. Bose agrees that for some veterans, admitting they have PTSD is considered a strike against their manhood. "There are macho guys who go into war. There's a culture of macho-ness, and they have to go out there and not show weakness. They come back and find they need help, and they can't face that. It really puts the onus on the family to recognize it and encourage the person to seek help."

The Culture of War

Even those tasked with carrying out the bloody details of war know the toll it takes on the men and women who follow them into battle. General William Tecumseh Sherman once advised that the glory of war "is all moonshine. It is only those who have neither fired a shot nor heard the shrieks and groans of the wounded who cry aloud for blood, for vengeance, for desolation. War is hell."

Gen. Sherman, a U.S. Civil War Union Army leader, is best known for the battle dubbed "Sherman's March." From Nov. 15 through Dec 21, 1864, Gen. Sherman and his 60,000 men marched 285 miles from Atlanta to Savannah, Georgia, in a campaign designed to frighten residents into no longer supporting the Confederacy.

Seventy-four years later, another general would espouse the horrors of war as he led his troops into the Southwest Pacific during World War II. "The soldier, above all others prays for peace, for it is the soldier who must suffer and bear the deepest wounds and scars of war," said Gen. Douglas MacArthur.

The realization that "war is hell" did not start with the Civil War. History books tell the story of individuals, states and political factions engaging in battle to gain sovereignty over other regions and peoples. One of the first recorded wars occurred in 2334 BCE in Mesopotamia, following a unification effort led by the leader of the Akkadian Empire. (Source: Ancient History Encyclopedia)

As long as war has existed, PTSD has been an unfortunate side effect. The condition has been labeled differently over the years, mostly by physicians trying to understand the signs, symptoms and underlying cause in a quest to help those returning from war.

During the Civil War, military physicians dubbed it "soldier's heart," because they noticed that returning soldiers were suffering from fear and stress as a result of their military service. As part of their medical evaluation, physicians noticed these soldiers had higher than normal blood pressure and heart rates. (Da Costa, J.M. (1871) Art. I-On irritable heart; A clinical study of a form of functional cardiac disorder and its consequences. American Journal of the Medical Sciences, 121(1), 2-52).

During World War I, doctors renamed the condition "shell shock" due to the dazed and disoriented state of soldiers who were afflicted with it. They believed the cause to be from concussions suffered from the impact of shells during periods of combat. Soldiers who were diagnosed with "shell shock" often were shunned by superiors and shamed back into active duty under the belief that real men didn't hide from their responsibility to serve their country. It wasn't until the war was nearly over that psychiatrists changed their minds about the condition, determining that it was the result of emotional problems rather than a physical injury to the brain that prompted the symptoms associated with "shell shock." (Scott, W.J. (1990) PTSD in the DSM-III: A case in the politics of diagnosis and disease. Social Problems, 37(3), 294-310).

During World War II, the scope of battle brought with it the risk of encountering bigger bombs and field weapons than American soldiers had ever experienced. Records from that time indicate that more than 25 percent of WWII casualties could be attributed to war trauma. Doctors tried out several names for the condition associated with wartime service before settling on "battle fatigue." Prior to that terminology, they also coined it as "combat neurosis" and "combat exhaustion." (Magee, D. (2006, May 15) PTSD: Only the name has changed. WCF Courier).

It wasn't until 1952 that the condition first appeared in the American Psychological Associations' Diagnostic and Statistical Manual of Mental Disorders I (DSM-1) under the name "gross stress reaction." The DSM indicated that the condition was believed to be the direct result of combat-related stress. But the label did not last for long. When the DSM-II was published in 1968, the condition had been entirely removed from the manual without explanation. (Andreasen, N.C. (2004) Acute and delayed posttraumatic stress disorders: A history and some issues. The American Journal of Psychiatry, 161, 1321-1323).

Terminology for the condition reappeared during the Vietnam Conflict, during which time it was renamed "Vietnam Combat Reaction" as a means to describe the 30.9 percent of returning war veterans suffering from insomnia, recurrent and terrifying nightmares, eating disorders, depression, feelings of guilt and extreme anxiety. (Price, J. L. (2007) Findings from the National Vietnam Veterans' Readjustment Study).

It wasn't until 1972, when a psychiatrist by the name of Chaim Shatan penned an article for the *New York Times* that described the disorder that it became known as "Post Vietnam Syndrome."

The article received tremendous support from the psychological community, which then prompted the taskforce responsible for the DSM to research the condition further. The taskforce re-labeled it "Catastrophic Stress Disorder." The term Post Traumatic Stress Disorder, or PTSD, was not coined until 1980, when the American Psychiatric Association added the term to the DSM-III.

Further revisions were made to the DSM to reflect the ongoing research into PTSD. The most recent version, DSM-V, was released in 2013, and no longer considers PTSD to be an anxiety disorder. It places PTSD in a new category called Trauma and Stressor Related Disorders. The DSM-V lists four types of symptoms commonly associated with PTSD: reliving the traumatic event; avoiding situations that are reminders of the event; negative changes in beliefs and feelings; and feelings of hyper-arousal (over-reaction to situations). The DSM-V requires all four symptoms to be present in order for PTSD to be properly diagnosed in an individual.

The Battle for Acceptance

Choosing a name and officially publishing it in the sacred diagnostic manual used by psychiatrists, psychologists and physicians was just the first step toward tackling PTSD. Knowing it exists is a far cry from helping veterans to accept they may have PTSD – and for those in their lives to be accepting of the changes that PTSD causes in their loved ones.

A common coping mechanism in most support groups is centered around theologian Reinhold Niebuhr's Serenity Prayer: God grant me the serenity to accept the things I cannot change, courage to change the things I can, and wisdom to know the difference.

Patrick is fully aware of most of the things that trigger him, and to avoid those triggers, he avoids the kinds of social situations he previously enjoyed immensely. "PTSD, and the overreaction to normal, everyday things that I have because of it, is the reason I am mostly a recluse now. I am wired for sound and ready to go and putting myself into a situation that most people would enjoy usually ends badly for me."

The Madrids, whom we first met back in Chapter 3, said accepting that PTSD was now a part of their lives was a major stepping stone toward tackling the issue and moving forward together. The realization that Joe Madrid has been diagnosed with PTSD is something that affects how they conduct themselves in their everyday lives.

"My son plays pro football, and I used to go to his games, but I can't anymore, because it's a huge trigger for me," said Joe Madrid. Crowds and especially large crowds of people drinking alcohol create an atmosphere he has trouble processing, so anything where those two things mix is something he avoids. "It's hard, but I've accepted it. It took a lot for my family to come around and to understand, but they get it now."

"You have to choose every day how you're going to act and how you're going to react," said Janine Madrid. "We have accepted there are some things we're just not going to be able to do anymore because they can be triggers for Joe, and there are other times when we have to be brave enough to see behind the façade and help him work through a situation. It's important for him and for anyone with PTSD to know they're not alone. There are other people who are going through this and there are people who are going to help them get through it."

Not everyone is able to cope with seeing a loved one battling the effects of PTSD. Some veterans lose their jobs, because employers and coworkers don't understand their behaviors. Some family members walk away because they either can't – or won't – deal with the new reality that is living with someone with PTSD.

Veteran Tim McKernan said he devoted 27 years to the military, retiring in March 2013. In January of 2003, he was deployed to Kuwait out of Fort Carson, Colo. While there, he was responsible for planning and executing the logistics of the attack on Iraq. He was stationed at Logistics Base Seitz in Balad, which was home to the 13th Corps Support Command. The base was attacked more than once during the Gulf War. McKernan later was deployed to Afghanistan for several tours and was there during the surge that lasted from October 2007 through January 2009. His last tour in the Middle East was from June 2009 through May 2010, when he was stationed in Baghdad, Iraq. He believes it was his time in Afghanistan that resulted in his PTSD.

"My career ended on a pretty sour note," he said. "My retirement award was mailed to me a month late. Since then, I've been unable to work, and my marriage of 24 years has ended. My dealings with the VA have been less than stellar and I struggled to get the help I needed for a long time."

It wasn't until July 2015 that he finally received Social Security Disability status, and also has been labeled as "100 percent unemploy-able" by the Veterans Administration. McKernan said his therapy dog and a return to his Catholic faith have helped him a lot on the road to recovery. "I can say without a doubt that was what kept me from taking my own life."

Both Joe Madrid, and John Vaughn, whom we first met in Chapter 3, said veterans who are struggling and find themselves without the support of friends or family members, need to reach out to other veterans who are experiencing the same thing.

"PTSD is a hard thing to explain to someone who has never experienced it. You can try to explain it to your family and friends, but even if they are sympathetic, they might still not be able to understand it. When that happens, it's really helpful to reach out to another vet who also is going through it, or a professional who can help you to work through it," said Madrid.

"It's important to remember you're not the only one going through this," said Vaughn. "There are other guys who are going through it and they get it."

Families who do wish to work through the stress of helping a loved one cope with PTSD may find family counseling and other types of therapy helpful. We discuss these options further in Chapter Nine, so read on or skip to that section now for further information.

Section III
Finding Their Way

****

"A journey of a thousand miles begins with a single step."
~Lao Tzu

****

CHAPTER NINE
Traditional Therapy and Treatment Options for PTSD

§

"A mental stain can neither be blotted out by the passage of time nor washed away by any waters."
~*Cicero*

Countless books on the market today discuss, in depth, what PTSD is and how it is diagnosed. This book also has spent some time discussing the clinical definition – as well as the physical and emotional manifestation – of PTSD. While it is important to understand how someone develops PTSD, and which signs and symptoms are an indicator that you – or someone you know – may have PTSD, it also is crucial to provide resources designed to help individuals and families who are living with PTSD. This chapter will discuss some of the more standard treatments for PTSD.

Talking it Out

Almost every veteran who has been diagnosed with PTSD has received a recommendation from their healthcare provider to attend individual or group therapy, sometimes both. Talking through the issues surrounding PTSD and forming a bond with others who know exactly what they are going through, is considered to be a tried and true first step in processing a PTSD diagnosis.

The National Center for PTSD has researched extensively types of therapy, including the effectiveness of each. The Veterans Affairs/Department of Defense PTSD Clinical Practice Guideline (CPG) for Posttraumatic Stress Disorder (2017), supports individual, trauma-focused psychotherapy as one of the preferred methods for treating PTSD. The center classifies the following techniques as approved methods under the trauma-focused psycho-therapy recommendation: prolonged exposure; cognitive processing therapy; and eye movement desensitization and reprocessing (EMDR).

The guidelines advise that the benefits of this kind of therapy last longer than the improvements associated with medication. If medication is prescribed in addition to therapy, the following are listed as the most effective: sertraline, paroxetine, fluoxetine and venlafaxine (Source: Clinician's Guide to Medications for PTSD).

One of the many purposes of individual and group therapy for veterans with PTSD is the idea that telling – and retelling – the story of the trauma that caused their PTSD in a safe space is a way to take ownership of the situation, thereby reducing its impact on the psyche. A significant number of studies have been conducted on the effectiveness of this kind of exposure-based treatment, with evidence suggesting that those who participate in this kind of therapy experience a reduction of PTSD symptoms. The therapy method was more successful in female veterans with PTSD than their male counterparts.

Patrick said he found value in sharing his story with other veterans who are dealing with PTSD, forming a sort of brotherhood with the men in his group therapy sessions. While therapy had its benefits, Patrick said he did not feel as if it was helping some of his bigger issues from the PTSD, such as reacting angrily to certain triggers while in public. "It was great to be able to share my thoughts and my struggles with others going through it but talking about it only helps so much."

Angel Mojica, whom we met in Section I of the book, said group therapy was especially helpful for him. He joined a group of veterans with similar combat experiences, and they decided to name their therapy group Global War on Terrorism since they all served in the Gulf at the same time. He said being able to talk to others who had "been there and done that" was the most beneficial thing he has done to treat his PTSD. "It was a good feeling to know I had a group of people who understood what I was going through and were there for me."

The Madrids, whom we met earlier in the book, have received therapy to help them deal with Joe Madrid's PTSD both as a couple, and as individuals. Janine Madrid said the intensive therapy they received as a couple and as individuals gave her the tools she needed to support her husband and to stay in their marriage. "And this may sound strange if you're not a believer, but I gave a lot of this up to God and for me, it helped immensely."

Joe Madrid said that counseling was good for him and he encourages other vets with PTSD to seek it out. But the program he feels truly made a difference was an intensive, one-and-a-half month stay in a mental health rehabilitation program sponsored by the VA. The program is located in St. Cloud, Minnesota, and only veterans who are referred by a treating physician are eligible to participate.

"It was a last resort for me. You have to kind of be on your knees before you're willing to do it; but I truly believe that program saved my life."

Janine Madrid agreed, saying "for Joe, it was a total healing, and not just from the PTSD."

Patrick can attest to the effectiveness of the in-treatment program in St. Cloud; he was prescribed a 30-day visit to the facility in January 2017. Patrick completed what was described as "phase one" of the program; an additional six-weeks will be scheduled for another time in order to finish "phase two." Because he is still working full time, Patrick has to schedule the intensive, resident treatment program when he is able to request enough time off work.

Phase one of the program focuses on everyday interactions with people, in what Patrick affectionately labeled "Dealing with People 101." He learned proven techniques to help him assess situations, people's intentions and behaviors and how his own guilt and shame over his PTSD can affect his everyday interactions with others. "I like the fact that the courses repeated throughout the cycle, so it helped to reinforce the lessons you already learned. But the only way this works is if you have a real issue with a real problem, and most of those are pretty embarrassing to talk about, which is where the emotional training portion of the program comes into play. It was the intensity of the training I received – the in-your-face, 24/7 aspect – that is key to it being effective. You have no choice but to face it, which is the first step in coping with it."

Changing the Behavior

One of the most beneficial coping mechanisms Patrick said he learned as part of his 30-day treatment program in St. Cloud is something known as Cognitive Behavioral Therapy.

According to the American Psychological Association, Cognitive Behavioral Therapy (CBT), is a form of psychological treatment that has been proven effective for conditions such as depression, anxiety disorders, alcohol and drug abuse, marital problems, eating disorders and severe mental illness. Studies suggest CBT results in significant improvement in the quality of life and overall functioning of a person with any of the listed conditions, including PTSD.

A specialized, manualized style of CBT, known as Cognitive Processing Therapy, was developed specifically with PTSD in mind. It has been so effective in treating veterans with PTSD that it is now one of the top two recommendations for initial treatment, according to Samantha S. Supernaw, a licensed therapist and clinical supervisor in private practice at Heart and Head Healing in Pflugerville, Texas. CPT has consistently reduced what she refers to as the use of "stuck points," which affect emotional output of those with PTSD. "(CPT) helps them process the trauma in a healthy way."

Supernaw has received specialized training in order to offer her clients CPT. The specialized training is incredibly comprehensive and designed to help therapists use the tenants of CPT effectively in patients who are dealing with trauma-related psychological conditions.

In order to complete the training, Supernaw was required to attend a two-day seminar, where she learned techniques to employ with her patients. She also was required to undergo six months of weekly consults and additional training with an expert in CPT, and work with five veterans who have been diagnosed with PTSD, or their family members.

The therapy is especially helpful in veterans who are dealing with feelings of survivor's guilt in addition to the PTSD. "(This therapy) looks at the belief system about why and how the trauma occurred and how it's still affecting them," said Supernaw. "I've found that with my patients with PTSD, the belief system directly impacts how they process the trauma. So, if someone feels responsible for the incident that led to their PTSD, guilt is part of the belief system and can make it difficult to resolve those feelings."

Many veterans with PTSD also are dealing with feelings of survivor's guilt. The story of how they developed their PTSD often involves them surviving an engagement with the enemy in which their friends and fellow soldiers were lost. For Patrick, his guilt over allowing Sgt. Williams to come on a mission in Iraq that ultimately cost him his life plays a huge role in how he processes his PTSD. The first phase of treatment he received during his residential treatment program in St. Cloud addressed his feelings of shame and guilt over living through an event that cost fellow soldiers their lives. "The only way this (treatment) works is if you have a real issue with a real problem – and most of those are pretty embarrassing to talk about – which is where the emotional training is helpful."

Patrick said that he had tried CPT before in individual therapy, but found it wasn't as effective as when he was going through it at the in-house treatment facility. "I think the difference in why it worked better at St. Cloud was because of the intensity of the training. It's in-your-face, 24/7, and you have no choice but to face it."

CPT also helped him with impulse control, which is something his PTSD overrides on a regular basis. "It was all about learning to identify, in the moment, that you are being triggered by a situation, and how to control your reaction to being triggered without blowing your lid over it." He also learned how to change his attitude to help prevent some of the "boiling over" moments of anger he had previously experienced over seemingly normal stressors.

Shortly after completing this phase of the in-house treatment program, Patrick said his new skills were put to the test when he experienced difficulty when dropping off his truck for servicing at a repair shop. "When I went back to get it, I found out they hadn't even done the work yet because the parts they originally ordered were wrong. So, I had been inconvenienced by being without my vehicle all day, and the work hadn't even been done. Instead of flipping out, like I would have done before, I applied what I learned (about CPT) and was able to stay calm. I felt really good about how I handled that entire situation."

Another issue that CPT addresses effectively is the bravado that keeps many veterans – especially males – from seeking help. "Veterans are concerned they look weak if they have to discuss any kind of trauma or mental health issue," said Supernaw. "What I like to tell my patients is there is no difference between PTSD and Type I Diabetes. We make these artificial distinctions between mental health problems and physical health problems, but to our brain, they are processed the exact same way. PTSD, especially, is a normal reaction to an abnormal, life-threatening situation."

Effectiveness of CPT is dependent on the way the therapy is applied, as well as the attitude and participation of the patient. The first phase of CPT – as Patrick experienced at St. Cloud – is designed to focus on the "blame game" and perception issues surrounding PTSD. The sooner a veteran seeks out help and begins phase one, the more likely they are to be successful with CPT, said Supernaw. "The longer people avoid dealing with their PTSD, the longer it will take for them to shed those bad habits. But once a patient can move past the 'what if' phase of dealing with the trauma, then the healing can begin."

The second phase of CPT focuses on safety, trust, control and self-esteem, said Supernaw. "A lot of people with PTSD really struggle with trust issues. That is absolutely normal."

The length of CPT therapy differs for each individual, said Supernaw. CPT is designed to be a 12-session treatment when receiving it through individual therapy sessions. "Some clients aren't going to need as many as 12 sessions and some are going to need more. Some are going to be more stuck than others. Some clients are more invested in challenging their avoidance of dealing with the PTSD and their determination helps with therapy."

As with many forms of therapy, some veterans may have concerns over paying for CPT. The Veterans Administration lists CPT as an approved therapy, and offers it at many of its facilities. Tricare, a health insurance program for active and retired military members and their families, also covers CPT.

Interactive Desensitization Therapy

While CPT forces an individual with PTSD to confront their condition head on in order to control it, Eye Movement Desensitization and Reprocessing (EMDR) uses a technique that requires an individual to relive traumatic or triggering experiences in small doses while a therapist redirects their eye movements.

There are eight phases of treatment involved with EMDR (American Psychological Association, Clinical Practice Guideline). They are:
•   Phase One: a full history of the patient will be obtained by their therapist, which can include talking about the trauma which caused the PTSD and identifying which memories require specific treatment.
•   Phase Two: the therapist will provide the patient with multiple ways to cope with the emotional or psychological stress experienced as part of the PTSD. Controlled breathing and mindfulness are among the techniques that may be used.
•   Phase Three: the therapist will assess and identify specific memories to be targeted during EMDR treatment, as well as any physical components that accompany PTSD triggers.
•   Phases Four through Seven: this is when the active treatment begins. The therapist will use EMDR techniques to treat the memories that were targeted in phase three. During the sessions, patients are asked to focus on a negative thought, memory or image. While the patient is focusing on the negative thought, memory

or image, the therapist will have the patient complete specific eye movements, which also may include bilateral stimulation such as taps or other movements. After the bilateral stimulation, the therapist will ask the patient to allow their mind to draw a blank in order to better grasp the thoughts and feelings that are being experienced. The therapist may then have the patient refocus on the traumatic memory or thought that occurred, or may move on to another.

• Phase Eight: Patients are asked to evaluate the progress they've made during active treatment to determine if it was successful.

Developed by American psychologist Francine Shapiro, Ph.D., in the late 1980s, EMDR has proven quite effective in helping veterans to overcome the devastating trauma of war (Behavioral Interventions, Volume 25, Issue 1, February 2010). It is believed to be effective because recalling distressing events when one's attention is diverted is less emotionally taxing. When repeated over time, EMDR can lessen the impact the traumatic memories have on an individual. If EMDR therapy has worked, the individual with PTSD will be able to reprocess traumatic events and information in a way that is no longer psychologically disruptive to their everyday life.

Patrick said he tried EMDR therapy through the VA when he was first diagnosed with PTSD and felt like it would have worked if he had been able to continue with the process. "When you come out of the EMDR, you feel like you've slept for 12 hours. It's very relaxing and calming."

Joe Madrid also tried EMDR therapy in 2007 and said it was helping, but the psychologist who was administering the treatments left the VA facility where he was being treated, and he had to stop.

Eva Foster, who we met in an earlier chapter, said EMDR is only successful if the individual receiving it is able to fully relive the trauma that resulted in their PTSD. "It's too much for some people, because they have to relive the event, which is necessary to make the process work. A lot of soldiers won't talk about the event in full detail – they only give the highlights. So, if they can't relive the trauma, they can't complete the process."

In her opinion, the most effective treatment would be a combination of CPT and EMDR. "The VA doesn't treat PTSD like it should," said Foster. "PTSD needs to be a multi-disciplinary treatment, not a one-size-fits-all. It needs to involve family members because they are technically experiencing secondary PTSD from walking on eggshells around us. Our families don't know what our triggers are . . . sometimes we don't even know."

EMDR therapy may not be available in some areas. To locate a therapist certified in the administration of EMDR therapy, visit www.emdr.com.

Trauma-Focused Therapy Options

In addition to CPT and EMDR, there are other types of trauma-focused therapies that the Veterans Administration and the National Center for PTSD recommend as options for the treatment of PTSD. They are:
• Brief Eclectic Psychotherapy (BEP) – this method encourages a veteran to practice relaxation skills while simultaneously re-

calling details of the traumatic event. The purpose of the therapy is to help veterans reframe negative thoughts associated with their trauma in order to overcome them.

• Narrative Exposure Therapy (NET) – this treatment method was developed for individuals who have experienced trauma from ongoing war, conflict or organized violence. It works by having the veteran talk through all of the stressful events they have experienced from birth to the present day, putting them together in an almost story format.

• Written Narrative Exposure – this form of therapy involves writing about the trauma during sessions with a therapist, who will give specific instructions on the writing assignment during each session. The veteran and therapist will then discuss the writing and address any negative symptoms associated with completing the exercise.

Medication Therapy

Medications are sometimes prescribed for the treatment of PTSD in veterans, sometimes alone, and sometimes in combination with other treatment methods like EMDR or CPT.

The National Center for PTSD has identified four antidepressant medications that it recommends in the treatment of PTSD in veterans: Sertraline (Zoloft); Paroxetine (Paxil); Fluoxetine (Prozac); and Venlafaxine (Effexor). These four antidepressants belong to the classification of medications known as SSRIs, or selective serotonin reuptake inhibitors, and SNRIs, or serotonin-norepinephrine reuptake inhibitors. SSRIs and SNRIs work by affecting the level of naturally-occurring chemicals in the brain called serotonin and norepinephrine, which are responsible for brain cell communication and can affect the way a person feels.

Veterans who are prescribed medication as part of treatment for PTSD will need to be monitored by a medical professional every few months to ensure the current dosage of medication is still adequately controlling unwanted symptoms and that no unwanted side effects are occurring.

In addition to therapy, Angel Mojica said was prescribed medication, which he described as helpful in managing his PTSD. Eva Foster said she also has medication, but only takes it when she feels she really needs it to control her symptoms.

Service Dogs and Emotional Support Animals

It is scientifically proven that pets are good for our health. Numerous studies cite the health benefits of owning a pet, including reduction in stress and anxiety. With that kind of evidence behind pet ownership, it only makes sense that it would be explored as an option for veterans with PTSD.

Veterans may have a service dog for physical needs resulting from war-related injuries or other medical conditions, while others may have emotional support dogs for emotional needs. There is a difference between a service dog – which is specially trained to assist in daily tasks – and emotional support dogs, which require no special training. Service dogs can be trained to pick things up, guide a person or help someone maintain their balance. Training for service dogs usually includes teaching them to complete tasks that are different from natural dog behavior (turning on lights or opening doors); complete tasks that the dog handler/owner cannot do because of a disability; and learn to work with their new handler/owner to help them better manage their disability. Because they depend on their service animals to complete everyday living tasks, service dogs are allowed to accompany their owners to most public places, including restaurants.

Emotional support dogs are tasked specifically with assisting their owners with mental health needs and require no special training in order to complete their duties. All that is required is for a mental health professional to write a recommendation saying their patient requires an emotional support animal, and any animal can be designated as such. However, emotional support animals do not have the same rights as service dogs and therefore may not be permitted to accompany their owners to public places like restaurants and stores.

Tim McKernan, who was introduced earlier in the book, has a miniature poodle as his emotional support dog. She is trained to distract him when he is becoming anxious. "She is trained to literally force me to hold her, so I am distracted from whatever else was making me upset. I have to focus on her instead of my anxieties."

McKernan said reaction to his emotional support animal is mixed; mostly, people find it hilarious. "People laugh when they see her, because miniature poodles are not your typical (emotional support) dog. But she used to be my daughter's dog, and we had a good relationship already established, so transitioning her into this role just made sense."

Retired Army Major Yancy Baer has become quite familiar with service dogs and the rights and responsibilities that come with owning one. Maj. Baer suffered an injury to his left leg while serving in Iraq. During surgery for that injury, doctors discovered a tumor in that leg that was previously undetected and had to amputate his leg to save his life. He now wears a prosthetic on that leg. Maj. Baer applied for a service dog through Canine Companions for Independence (CCI), a national organization that has been pairing service dogs with veterans with disabilities since 1975. His dog, Verbena, has been with him for five years. She received two years of intensive training with CCI before being paired with Maj. Baer.

CCI breeds its own dogs for the program, which are Labrador-Golden Retriever mixes. CCI has discovered that the mixed-breed dogs are better at performing the kinds of tasks needed by many who use service dogs. "It's the best of both worlds," Maj. Baer said of his dog, which he affectionately calls "Beanz" for short. "They have the personality of a Retriever, and the work ethic of a Lab."

CCI's dogs begin training as service animals as young as eight weeks, learning basic tasks. Once they reach six months of age, dogs begin training for more complicated tasks. Maj. Baer said he has a lot of issues with his back due to the amputated leg, some of which make it difficult for him to bend over to retrieve things. "That's what Beanz does for me, especially first thing in the morning." Before he even gets out of bed, Beanz will bring him items he needs, sometimes even including his prosthetic leg. "If I leave the things I want her to bring to me first thing in a certain place, she just automatically knows to bring them. That's part of her training. She also picks things up for me, so I don't have to bend over or bend down a lot, which hurts my back."

While having a service dog has been a huge help to him, Maj. Baer said there are responsibilities that come with having Beanz. Chief among those responsibilities is knowing his rights to public access. In 2014, Maj. Baer experienced the kind of misinformation about service animals that ended up gaining national attention in the media when an employee for a well-known coffee chain tried to deny him service because of Beanz. The irony of the situation was that Maj. Baer was in town on behalf of CCI and two of the representatives from the organization were with him when he encountered the difficulty gaining entry into the coffee chain with his dog. "At first, I thought the (employee) was joking around, because when I told him that Beanz was my service dog, he insisted she couldn't be a service dog because I wasn't blind. He then asked me what she did for me if she was my service dog, and I told him, and his response was 'well, why can't you do that stuff for yourself?' It became quickly clear that he had no idea what my rights are as a service dog owner."

The employee's first mistake was to deny Maj. Baer entry with his service animal. The second mistake was asking what tasks the dog performed to make it a service animal. Both are considered a violation of the Americans with Disabilities Act (ADA).

Maj. Baer said the situation continued to escalate because other patrons came to his defense. Rather than leave the establishment, he said he decided to make it a learning opportunity for everyone. He followed the protocol that is recommended for anyone with a service animal who is refused service while the animal is with them.

First, he asked to speak to the manager of the coffee shop. The employee said the manager was unavailable, but Maj. Baer was able to speak to another employee who was more understanding and explained to the other employee that service dogs were permitted in the coffee shop. The first employee later apologized to him for the misunderstanding. "This incident is what really triggered me to get to know more about my rights as a service dog owner and it is something I tell every person with a service dog that they should do."

There are recommended steps that an individual with a service dog should take if they are ever in this same situation. As Maj. Baer demonstrated, the first step is always to ask to speak to a manager and remind them the ADA provides for individuals to be accompanied by their service animals in all public places, including restaurants. If a manager is not available, or also is unaware of your rights and continues to deny access, contact the local police to assist. In addition to the ADA, some states also have laws pertaining to access that may provide additional protections. In Texas, where the incident with Maj. Baer occurred, a law (House Bill 489) had recently been passed that made denying access to a disabled person with a service animal a misdemeanor offense with applicable fines attached to the violation. Even when local or state provisions are not in place, police officers are permitted to remind business owners of the provisions of the federal ADA, which carry civil penalties. The maximum civil penalty for a first violation under the ADA is $75,000; subsequent violations can incur a maximum penalty of $150,000. (March 28, 2014 Department of Justice Final Ruling)

In addition to the ADA and individual state laws pertaining to disability rights, there also are protections afforded under the following at the national level which apply to individuals who use a service animal:

• Fair Housing Act of 1968 – which includes amendments of 1988 – provides equal access to private housing, housing that accepts federal financial assistance, and state and local government housing.

• Rehabilitation Act of 1973 prohibits discrimination based on disability in programs that are conducted by federal agencies, in programs that receive federal financial assistance, in federal employment and in the employment practices of federal contractors.

• Air Carrier Access Act of 1986 provides protections for passengers traveling with disabilities and includes provisions pertaining to service animals.

While service dog owners may carry certification from the organization where they obtained their service animal, businesses and individuals are not permitted to ask for that certification as evidence of the service animal's right to public access. Some service dogs wear vests identifying them as service animals. While this is not a requirement for public access, Maj. Baer said it is a good idea to have your service dog wear one for a number of reasons. "The first thing people do when they see a dog is they get excited, then the dog gets excited, which can distract the dog from its purpose. If dogs are distracted, especially ones trained to perform tasks such as seeing eye dogs or those trained to detect seizures, being distracted can result in a serious injury or maybe even death of the handler."

Service vests are available which indicate a handler's preference on their dog being approached by and interacting with (petting) the public.

Maj. Baer said while he doesn't mind people wanting to pet Beanz, he appreciates being asked first before any contact is made. The same consideration should be extended to any individual who is accompanied by a service animal. "And if you ask to pet the dog, and the person says no, don't be offended."

While some veterans with PTSD have emotional support dogs, Maj. Baer said CCI is leading the way in training dogs with specific tasks so that they may be classified as service dogs instead of emotional support animals, giving the handler more rights to public access while with the animal. The ADA requires that a dog be able to perform at least two specific tasks related to the individual's disability in order to qualify as a service animal. CCI has found a way to meet that requirement for those with PTSD and has a launched a pilot program to directly place service animals with veterans with PTSD. The dogs are trained to complete tasks including nightmare interruption, retrieval of items, turning lights on and off, and supporting the veteran in crowded public situations that can cause anxiety, which is common in individuals with PTSD. Veterans who struggle with being in crowded places can use their service dog as a barrier between them and close contact with others, Maj. Baer said.

Veterans who would like to learn more about the PTSD service dog program at CCI can find additional information in Chapter 12 of this book. Those who wish to learn more about Maj. Baer and Beanz can visit their Facebook page: https://www.facebook.com/You-Dont-Know-Beanz-268464979977650/.

CHAPTER TEN
Alternative Strategies for Treating PTSD

§

"What counts is not necessarily the size of the dog in the fight – but the size of the fight in the dog."
~Pres. Dwight D. Eisenhower

While many veterans have benefited from the kinds of PTSD therapy discussed in our previous chapter, there are some veterans who have found relief through what can only be considered some very non-traditional methods. Some of these alternative methods are considered to be less controversial than others; however, this chapter will explore a number of unconventional options for veterans who have sought – but not found relief for their PTSD – through more standard treatments.

Not Exactly Prescription Medication

During the last couple of years, several states have taken steps of legalizing marijuana. Some states have legalized it for recreational purposes, while others have legalized it only for medicinal purposes that require a physician's evaluation and approval before a patient can legally obtain marijuana.

As of May 2018, states that have legalized marijuana for recreational purposes include:
•   Alaska – it is legal for adults 21 and over to possess up to

one ounce of marijuana and legal to grow up to six marijuana plants per household.

- California – it is legal for adults 21 and over to possess up to one ounce and legal to grow up to six plants per household.
- Colorado – it is legal for adults 21 and over to possess up to one ounce of marijuana and legal to grow up to six plants per household.
- District of Colombia – it is legal for adults 21 and over to possess up to two ounces of marijuana and legal to grow up to six plants per household.
- Maine – it is legal for adults 21 and over to possess up to 2.5 ounces of marijuana and legal to grow up to three flowering plants per household.
- Massachusetts – it is legal for adults 21 and over to possess up to one ounce of marijuana and legal to grow up to six plants per household.
- Nevada – it is legal for adults 21 and over to possess up to one ounce of marijuana and legal to grow up to six plants per household.
- Oregon – it is legal for adults 21 and over to possess up to one ounce on their person and up to eight ounces at home. It is also legal to grow up to four plants per person.
- Vermont – it is legal for adults 21 and over to possess up to one ounce of marijuana and legal to grow up to six plants per household.
- Washington – it is legal for adults 21 and over to possess up to one ounce; however, it is illegal to grow your own plants.

As of May 2018, the following states allow only for the use of medical marijuana:

- Arizona
- Arkansas
- Connecticut
- Delaware
- Florida
- Hawaii
- Illinois
- Maryland
- Michigan
- Minnesota
- Montana
- New Hampshire
- New Jersey
- New Mexico
- New York
- North Dakota
- Ohio
- Pennsylvania
- Rhode Island
- West Virginia

So, how does marijuana help alleviate the symptoms associated with PTSD? Marijuana contains more than 120 active compounds; however, studies into the effectiveness of treating PTSD with marijuana have focused on just tetrahydrocanna-binol (THC) and cannabidiol (CBD). Marijuana's principal psychoactive ingredient is THC, and is the one most scientists have focused on in their studies because of its ability to bind to specific brain cell receptors that are responsible for regulating mood, sleep and pain perception. Studies also suggest that THC interacts with the receptors in the amygdala and hippocampus, considered to be the emotional "centers" of the brain.

A 2009 clinical trial in Canada concluded that administering THC to individuals before bedtime reduced the frequency and intensity of nightmares in 72 percent of the 47 patients involved in the trial. (Source: The Use of Synthetic Cannabinoid in the Management of Treatment-Resistant Nightmares in Posttraumatic Stress Disorder, George A. Fraser, 13 February 2009). The study also concluded that dosage of THC was critical to achieving a positive result. Lower doses improved the quality of the individual's sleep, while higher doses produced more intense levels of anxiety.

A September 2017 study published in the *Annals of Internal Medicine* titled "Benefits and Harms of Plant-Based Cannabis for Posttraumatic Stress Disorder: A Systematic Review," concluded that evidence was insufficient to determine the benefit or harm of using plant-based cannabis for the treatment of PTSD, especially over the long term.

Studies into the effectiveness of marijuana in the treatment of PTSD continue, some conducted by institutions and medical organizations, while others have been commissioned by the Veterans Affairs Administration. Whether marijuana may be a viable treatment is a decision best left to the individual and his or her healthcare provider. Veterans who have tried other forms of treatment without success may wish to discuss the option if medical marijuana has been approved for PTSD in their state.

States which allow medical marijuana have a process in place to review and approve candidates for a medical marijuana card that will allow that individual to obtain marijuana products from an authorized dispensary. Criteria differs by state, but generally includes a list of diagnosed conditions that are considered approved for treatment with medical marijuana. Individuals may be required to consult with a pre-approved physician, rather than their regular primary care doctor, for the medical marijuana eligibility process. Many states limit the number of physicians who are eligible to evaluate and prescribe medical marijuana to residents. To find out if medical marijuana covers PTSD in your state, visit your state's Department of Health and Human Services.

Marijuana isn't the only former street drug being considered for the treatment of PTSD. One of the most controversial, yet promising, alternative treatments for PTSD comes in the form of a little green pill known by the pharmaceutical name of methylenedioxymethamphetamine (MDMA). There is another name for this innovative treatment – one that is more commonly heard on the street: Ecstasy.

Using Ecstasy to enhance psychotherapy is hardly a new concept. It was first documented for use for that purpose in 1978. Since it was labeled as an illegal substance in the U.S. in the 1980s, it was difficult for researchers to fully explore its effectiveness. When the Food and Drug Administration (FDA) approved the first clinical trial for MDMA nearly a decade later, theories for the use of the drug began to surface and included its ability to help induce positive moods and suppress negative thoughts that individuals may have during psychotherapy treatment. (Source: Clinical Psychology Review, "Emerging Treatments for PTSD, Judith Cukor, Josh Spitalnick, JoAnn Difede, Albert Rizzo and Barbara O. Rothbaum). Another study, published in the British journal The Lancet Psychiatry in May 2018, concluded that 68 percent of patients who received MDMA after just two sessions of psychotherapy saw dramatic decreases in their PTSD symptoms. The trial included 26 patients, the majority of which were combat veterans and first responders diagnosed with chronic PTSD who had not had success with other PTSD treatments.

Based on this and other recent studies, the FDA recently has granted MDMA a breakthrough therapy status, which could aid in speeding up the approval of the use of the drug for legal use by 2021. It is important to note that, even if MDMA receives final approval by the FDA for widespread usage in the medical community, it is intended to be used in conjunction with other forms of psychotherapy and not as a stand-alone treatment. The concept of using MDMA centers around its administration shortly before a psychotherapy session so that the patient will be more relaxed and able to handle discussing and reliving traumatic moments in order to process them with their therapist. Being able to recount the trauma is an important step in any psychotherapy treatment.

The use of MDMA with psychotherapy methods such as prolonged exposure may be especially beneficial. Prolonged exposure is a form of cognitive behavioral therapy and is considered to be one of the most effective treatments for PTSD. (Source: Foa et al., 1999, 2005; 2018; Powers et al., 2010; Resick et al., 2002; Rothbaum et al., 2005; Schnurr et al., 2007). Sessions generally range between 60 and 90 minutes, with most psychiatric professionals recommending between eight and 15 sessions.

Prolonged exposure consists of four main treatment components:
• Repeated exposure to situations the individual is avoiding due to trauma-related feelings and fears;
• Prolonged visitation of the memories of the trauma, paired with the therapist helping the individual to discuss the experience and process thoughts that are unhelpful to coping with the trauma;
• Education about the common reactions individuals have to trauma; and
• Learning breathing techniques that help the individual regain composure and/or remain calm when confronted with situations which trigger their PTSD.

By pairing MDMA with the hallmark tenants of prolonged exposure, researchers believe the combination will provide a powerful one-two punch, helping individuals to more easily withstand, in particular, phase two of prolonged exposure therapy.

Focus the Body, Free the Mind

The use of former street drugs isn't the only way veterans can learn to free their minds enough to find peace from their PTSD.

Yoga is a common form of exercise recommended to individuals dealing with any kind of anxiety issue, including PTSD. But Mars, Pa. resident Maggi Aebi takes the traditional yoga one step further with her iRest Inspired Meditation practice. The iRest form of yoga was developed by Richard Miller, Ph.D., a clinical psychologist and founder, executive director and president of the board of directors for the Integrative Restoration Institute. iRest is based on ancient yogic teachings with a modern-day twist that allows practitioners to tap into the parts of their brains that are responsible for thoughts, feelings and sensations. Miller claims that those who practice iRest regularly can learn how to respond to, rather than react to, challenging situations. Clinical studies also have supported the findings that iRest decreases stress, anxiety, fear and depression; improves sleep and reduces bouts of insomnia; helps with the management of chronic and acute pain; encourages increased energy levels; and an improved sense of control. (Source: Comparative Effectiveness of Three Occupational Therapy Sleep Interventions: A Randomized Controlled Study, 2016. Sharon A. Gut-man, Kristin A. Gregory, Megan M. Sadlier-Brown, Marcy A. Schlissel, Allison M. Schubert, Lee Ann Westover, and Richard C. Miller).

Aebi first learned of iRest when she was suffering from a tumor and meningitis, which affected her physically and emotionally. Several years later, after going through the end of her marriage and the loss of her son – Staff Sergeant Edward F. Greiner Jr., who died in an accident outside of Fort Bragg, N.C., where he was stationed with the 82nd Airborne Division awaiting deployment to Afghanistan – she rediscovered how iRest could help her through her grief. After successfully using iRest to combat her personal demons, Aebi said she realized it could greatly benefit veterans, including those with PTSD. "I wanted to take my tragedy, and turn it into something that could help someone else." So, she began to receive additional training that would allow her to use her yoga skills with that specific purpose in mind. She attended a yoga and trauma workshop conducted by David Emerson, author of "Yoga for Trauma." Emerson and Bessel van der Kolk co-founded the Trauma Center, where they developed their Trauma Sensitive Yoga protocol. Aebi spent a week training in the method. "I came home with certification to teach this method of yoga and a passion for it."

She also attended a course offered by Warriors at Ease, where she received certification in the program. According to the Warriors at Ease website, it is "a global community of teachers committed to supporting the health and healing of veterans, service members and their families through yoga and meditation."

Aebi has taken the skills she has learned and used them to work with several support programs for veterans, including Wounded Warriors and Vets Leadership. In 2016, she opened her own studio, called Yoga on Mars, where she offered a once-weekly session specifically for veterans. "I see things change, from the minute they walk into the room until they leave," said Aebi of the veterans who have tried the program. "The meditation process is amazing when they are open to doing it."

She also has launched a nonprofit called Healing 4 Heroes Hearts, which is dedicated to providing free access to trauma-sensitive yoga and meditation classes for veterans with PTSD and their families. To learn more about the program, visit https://healing4heroeshearts.org.

Working up a Sweat

A number of studies have shown that yoga and meditation can be helpful for those dealing with PTSD; however, similar studies have supported the positive effects associated with cardiovascular exercise in the reduction of PTSD symptoms.

Researchers at the University of Regina provided evidence that suggests aerobic exercise has "anxiolytic effects" on those with PTSD or other anxiety disorders. In layman's terms, cardiovascular exercise inhibits anxiety. The researchers studied the effects of cardiovascular exercise in controlled conditions for 33 PTSD-affected participants, who were required to complete two weeks of stationary biking aerobic exercise for a total of six sessions. The participants were randomly assigned to one of three groups: group one focused on attention to somatic arousal by having participants receive prompts directing their attention to the effects of the exercise; group two focused on distraction from somatic arousal by having participants watch a nature documentary while exercising; and group three exercised without any interventions that would distract or prompt them in any way. While each group was targeted for a slightly different focus, researchers discovered that participants of the three groups achieved reduced PTSD and anxiety sensitivity following the two-week period. (Source: Aerobic Exercise Reduces Symptoms of Posttraumatic Stress Disorder: A Randomized Controlled Trial, Matthew G. Fetzner and Gordon J.G. Asmundson, 9 June 2014).

A team of researchers at Loughborough University in the United Kingdom also have reviewed several studies on the impact of sports and physical activity on combat veterans who were diagnosed with PTSD. The team's findings suggest that engaging in regular physical activity reduces the symptoms of PTSD, improves coping skills, and enhances overall well-being. (Source: Peter Harrison Centre for Disability Sport, Exercise as Medicine, Dr. Anthony Papthomas, Prof. Vicky Tolfrey, Emily Hunt, Prof. Brett Smith, Dr. Nick Caddick, and Toni Williams).

CrossFit trainer Ryan Cage of Davenport, Iowa - who was diagnosed with PTSD after a 2011 near-death work accident that left him with burns over 10 percent of his body – said he is living proof that regular physical exercise can help with PTSD. Cage is the owner of CrossFit Port Byron. He chose CrossFit to help manage his PTSD symptoms because of the nature of the program. "CrossFit consists of high-intensity, functional movements that are designed to confuse the body in different ways." In order to complete many of the movements of Cross-Fit, an individual must be focused on the routine, which can help to distract from the usual anxiety that is part of PTSD. "There is a great foundation (with CrossFit) for anyone with PTSD to work their body and their mind."

CrossFit also is ideal for veterans who may have physical injuries in addition to the PTSD diagnosis. Patrick began taking CrossFit with Cage following surgery on his shoulder for an on-going issue resulting from his injuries during the 2003 incident in Iraq. Cage said he modified CrossFit routines for Patrick to accommodate his physical injuries, but said he was seeing positive results in Patrick physically. Patrick also reports that the intense workouts have not only been great for his physical conditioning, but also his mental health. "It's been great for helping me to get out some of that pent-up frustration and anxiety that I feel almost all the time because of the PTSD."

At the time of the interview, Cage said Patrick was the first veteran with PTSD he had trained using CrossFit, but added that he hoped to use his personal experience to help others in the same situation. "Pat and I get along well, because we understand how each other feels," said Cage. "I went through something pretty intense that caused my PTSD, but I've always been the type of person to move forward instead of being impaired by the past. My wife says I'm stubborn, but I hope to use that to help others."

The Power of Positivity

While being stubborn may sometimes be a good character trait in the battle against PTSD, the power of positivity also plays a role in conquering the beast.

Angel Mojica, whom we met in an earlier chapter, has taken his PTSD and used it to help others just like him. "One of the many decisions the VA Center helped me make after I was diagnosed was to pursue a career where I could help others. I felt like my experience and my ability to understand where these guys were coming from would be an asset." As of the writing of this book, Mojica was serving as the Senior Vice Commandant of the Marine Corps League in his area. "My job is to help fellow Marines who need financial or other assistance." He also plans to use his position to help local veteran groups work collaboratively toward common goals, which will greatly increase their ability to serve the veteran population.

Like Cage, Corporal Brandon Rumbaugh of the U.S. Marines understands the concept of taking something awful and turning it into a positive opportunity. Cpl. Rumbaugh retired medically from military service in September 2012 following five years of active duty with the 1st Battalion 8th Marines as an 81mm mortar gunner. He was deployed to both Iraq and Afghanistan during his five years of active duty. He was 27 years old at the time of his retirement, which was necessary due to injuries suffered during a deployment to Afghanistan, where he suffered multiple injuries from an IED explosion. During a routine security patrol around their temporary outpost, one of his fellow Marines was injured by an IED. In his attempt to rescue the injured Marine, Cpl. Rumbaugh encountered a second IED just 25 meters from his wounded friend's position in the field. The impact of the IED resulted in the loss of both of his legs. While Cpl. Rumbaugh has not been diagnosed with PTSD, one of the many injuries he received during the IED explosion was a traumatic brain injury.

Cpl. Rumbaugh spent 16 months recovering from his injuries at Walter Reed, where he underwent extensive therapy. It would have been easy for Cpl. Rumbaugh to give up and become depressed at his new reality; but instead, he has chosen to take his situation and turn it into a way to not only motivate himself, but others. As part of this mission, he frequently retells the story of his service and of his injuries to veterans as part of his involvement with It's About the Warrior Foundation. "When I met Steve (Montelione), I realized that I was in a position to help other veterans, but also high school kids and other people as well. I don't consider what I do to be just motivational speaking. I've talked to elementary kids and CEOs of top companies. Sharing my experiences and what I've been through helps set people down the road toward success. They look at me and the obstacles I've had to overcome, and know that if I can do it, surely they can do it, too."

Although he works hard to stay positive, Cpl. Rumbaugh said that he would be lying if he didn't acknowledge that there are days when he needs someone to motivate him and keep him focused on his goals. "I never lie about that when I'm telling people my story. There is a fine line between being as open as possible, but not hiding the fact that I have flaws. I make sure they know I am not 100 percent every day. There are days I feel bad and feel sorry for myself, but that just makes me human."

He may not have PTSD, but Cpl. Rumbaugh has lived through a very traumatic experience. It can be just as difficult for him to re-count the events which led up to his life-changing injuries, but he said he does it because being able to help others by sharing his story gives him purpose and helps him to be thankful for being alive. "I am thankful for the fact that I'm alive and here right now, because so many of our men and women who fought and served are not."

Focusing on his goals also is a way to use his experience, rather than trying to forget about his trauma. "It's accepting it, dealing with it, and then moving on and finding something positive to focus on in your life. If you can do that, it will set you up for success in any situation."

CHAPTER ELEVEN
Heal the Soul, Heal the Mind
§

"People generally don't suffer high rates of PTSD after natural disasters. In-stead, people suffer from PTSD after moral atrocities. Soldiers who've endured the depraved world of combat experience their own symptoms. Trauma is an expulsive cataclysm of the soul."
~David Brooks

It can be an odd thing to hear a psychologist so readily discussing the effects of trauma on the human soul. The very term psychology was created by combining the Greek words psyche – meaning "breath, principle of life, life, soul" – and logia – meaning "speech, word, reason" and is used to describe the study of the human mind and its functions (Merriam Webster). But, that is exactly what happens when talking about PTSD and other trauma-related conditions with Dr. Roger Brooke, a licensed psychologist and Director of the Military Psychological Services at the Duquesne University Psychology Clinic.

It is not that Dr. Brooke does not believe in traditional psychotherapy methods, but rather that he believes they are inappropriate for the treatment of PTSD. "The specific skills and techniques that have been popular and recognized by my colleagues are fine and if people find them useful, that's great. The problem is the diagnosis of PTSD as a psychiatric condition is fundamentally misguided. What we call PTSD is our social construction treated as a psychotic issue. But the psychological wounds of war are essentially a spiritual issue."

An examination of the American Psychiatric Association's Diagnostic and Statistical Manual of Mental Disorders (DSM-5) supports his theory that the psychological community as a whole is not in the business of exploring or treating the effects of trauma on the soul. "There are no spiritual conditions listed in the DSM," said Dr. Brooke. "It ignores the moral and spiritual crises involved in killing and the witnessing of and participation in killing. It's a universal trauma."

Dr. Brooke's theories are very much Jungian in nature. Carl Jung, a Swiss psychiatrist and psychoanalyst, was credited with founding analytical psychology. He was known for his archetypal perspective and believed that while there was no limit to the number of archetypes that existed, there were four that existed within all human beings: the self, the shadow, the persona and the anima/animus. Jung believed the self was representative of the unconscious and conscious parts of the mind and was the central governing archetype of the human psyche. The shadow is what Jung called the deeper, darker elements of the human psyche, which includes repressed ideas, instincts, thoughts, weaknesses and desires. He believed the shadow was responsible for housing the human psyche's deepest thoughts and fears and that the persona is the public presentation of an individual to the outside world, which tends to be a bit of a disguise. Jung described the persona as humans giving their best impression to others and warned that mistaking our persona for our true selves can be a road block to successful therapy. The anima represents the feminine qualities of the male psyche, while the animus represents the masculine qualities in women. Jung believed the anima/animus to be the true representation of a human; it was considered to be the route to a person's soul and the source of their creativity.

Dr. Brooke said using a Jungian perspective in the search to relieve PTSD in combat veterans prompts psychology professionals to shift the focus from the mind to the soul by asking if there might be deeper meaning in combat PTSD symptoms. "Successful treatment involves helping the patient to understand PTSD isn't a mental illness, but a spiritual and moral condition. We need to ask the question, 'What does this PTSD want from me?' The things you can't forget have made a claim on you and you have to figure out why."

Some traditional cultures focus on the effects of trauma on the soul. The Plains Indians, which Dr. Brooke has studied, placed specific emphasis on the importance of the soul. They would give thanks to the buffalo or caribou they killed, taking responsibility for their dead spirit. What is lesser known, Dr. Brooke said, is that they also took responsibility for the souls of their enemies killed in battle as a way to spare themselves being haunted by them. "People with combat trauma are all haunted by images of the dead . . . dead friends, dead enemies . . . and there's a tremendous amount of guilt. Trying to convince them they shouldn't feel guilty is cutting that veteran off from his own humanity and deepening his despair."

Cultures that incorporate an acknowledgment of the stain that trauma leaves on the soul tend to have a better success rate in treating it, said Dr. Brooke. It is a method that could be especially effective for combat veterans. "They need to acknowledge that because of the trauma, they have been changed and can never go back to the civilian person they were before serving. The soldier-to-civilian idea is doomed to failure. They know that they're not the same and we need to honor that while helping them to start to live that difference with dignity and meaning."

Dr. Brooke said it is his belief that veterans battling PTSD will not truly find peace until they accept whatever lesson their service and the resulting trauma has for them. "This desire to forget about what happened is doomed to failure. It's not a good destiny. We need to take the lessons presented and make a difference, and this is not an easy task."

One of his patients, a Vietnam veteran, had been struggling with PTSD for many years before seeking help with Dr. Brooke. The veteran recounted his time as a U.S. Army Ranger, and told Dr. Brooke he had been tormented by the shooting of a Vietnamese woman. The veteran said he was forced to shoot her after she refused to stop when approaching him after several requests to do so. The woman had a straw hat concealing her midsection, and he was afraid she was armed. Those kinds of attacks on U.S. military members were not uncommon during the Vietnam Conflict. As it turned out, the woman was carrying a bomb. By shooting her, he saved the lives of fellow soldiers and other civilians nearby. "He had saved their lives, but he could not move past that one act. He had been to therapy for years, where he was told he had no reason to feel guilty. So, he asked me if he had no reason to feel guilty, then why does her face never leave him? Eventually, we came to the realization together that it was because he felt guilty not just because he had killed someone, but because he had shot and killed a woman. He was experiencing guilt more from a human standpoint, not from a soldier's standpoint. Guilt isn't a bad thing if you let it speak to you. That guilt is what saves your soul."

Dr. Brooke is not the only prominent psychology professional who believes that effective treatment of PTSD must involve the examination of trauma's effect on the soul. Dr. Edward Tick is known worldwide as a transformational healer. In the late 1970s, before PTSD was even a diagnostic category in the DSM, Dr. Tick was using psychotherapy treatment with Vietnam veterans who were experiencing the effects of war trauma. He is the co-founder and executive director of Soldier's Heart, a nonprofit organization which employs psychospiritual and cross-cultural healing methods with veterans suffering from military and war trauma. Dr. Tick's methods have proven so effective that he was invited to train 1,200 military chaplains and senior officials in the NATO in 2012. His methods and the justification for using them to treat PTSD can be found in several of Dr. Tick's books, including "War and the Soul" (2005) and "Warrior's Return" (2014).

In addition to the books he's written on the topic, Dr. Tick and his wife, Kate Dahlstedt, operate retreats and programs for veterans who wish to receive their unique treatment for PTSD. Dahlstedt, whom we met earlier in the book, holds a master's degree in clinical psychology and a post-graduate certification from the Hartford Family Institute. At present, she directs the Soldier's Heart Military Families Project and the Athena's Shield for Women Project.

"(Soldiers) are taught to act without thinking, which is what you have to do to survive in war," said Dahlstedt. "But then later, they realize what they have done. That enemy is someone with a family – a wife, children. And if their trauma involves a child, or an old woman – who are totally innocent – that can be even more damaging."

Providing our military members with sophisticated weaponry and teaching them how to use it effectively in a combat situation is a powerful adrenaline high, she said. "That's the feeling of the power of God in your hands, and that's too much for any human being to handle. So, we have to normalize these feelings and help them to realize they are not monsters."

Being in that position of protector or defender can cause identity confusion when soldiers return home to civilian life. It is why Dahlstedt said she believes a high percentage of veterans seek out careers as emergency responders when they return to civilian life, because they wish to continue in the role of defender or protector. As part of their treatment programs and retreats, Dahlstedt said she and Dr. Tick guide veterans toward creative and positive expressions that honor the continued desire to serve as protector or defender, while countering the destruction they participated in during active war time. "It's an antidote to feeling like you're nothing more than a destroyer."

The methods employed during Soldier's Heart retreats present a unique approach to contending with what Dr. Tick refers to as "the warrior experience." His methods help veterans to realize that PTSD is a normal and natural response to the experience of war trauma. Instead of focusing on PTSD as a pathology or disease to be treated, Dr. Tick instead presents it as a larger path that any warrior must follow by going through the following steps: isolation and tending; affirmation of warrior density; purification and cleansing; storytelling, restitution in the community; and initiation. Each phase of the program helps veterans come to terms with the fact that the warrior mentality is something that affects their spiritual, psychological, cultural, historical and social lives.

Dahlstedt said a crucial part of their therapy method is the connection to community, which occurs in the storytelling and restitution portions of the program. After studying other cultures and their practices, she and Dr. Tick discovered that the involvement of the community as a whole is a key factor in veterans learning to cope with the trauma of war. "People nowadays tend to be so apathetic, so when (Edward's) first book came out, we were amazed at the community response we started to receive. Sometimes it's a hard sell, especially for communities where they may have protested a war. But getting community members together with veterans can get the process of healing started for all of them. Our retreats get veterans together to talk openly about their experiences and to help the community to have understanding and compassion for our military."

Dr. Brooke, who has studied Dr. Tick's methodologies and has served as a leader at some of his retreats, said the storytelling component of the retreats is powerful for both veterans and civilians and is a necessary part of the soul-healing process. Listening to the trauma of war is a way for the community to help carry the burden of that trauma along with the veterans who have lived it, he said. "During storytelling, when our veterans are sharing their experiences, it is the civilians' turn to bear witness to the violence done in their name and to listen to the stories, no matter how painful it is for them to hear."

In his book, "War and the Soul," Dr. Tick also stresses the importance of guidance from others – particularly elders – who have been through similar experiences. He encourages elders to pass on their values, guidance, wisdom and experience to the younger initiates. Other cultures, such as the Plains Indians, engaged in this practice. Dr. Brooke supports this finding, noting that soldiers should be able to look to their military leaders to walk them through the trauma. In order for this to work, the stigma surrounding PTSD needs to be lifted and veterans need to be encouraged to talk openly about their experiences with one another.

While testimonials abound for the success of the unique approach Dr. Tick and Dr. Brooke have taken with veterans, Dr. Brooke cautioned that it is not a magic cure-all for PTSD. Psychiatric symptoms, such as the need to sit with their backs to a wall or avoiding crowds, may always be a part of the battle, but are symptoms which are entirely manageable, he said. "Being depressed and feeling betrayed are devastating to a person's character and can do far more damage. Some of the psychiatric symptoms at a psychological level will remain no matter what, but things like depression are drastically reduced when veterans claim it and own their identity as a warrior. The trauma of war will be passed on to the next generation no matter what. But this way allows it to be passed on as a story of remarkable men and the healing of the warrior with the community."

Chapter Twelve
Resources for PTSD

§

"We're all broken and damaged, and we aren't quite fixed yet. A lot of us have gone through hell, but you know what? We came back. We came back stronger. You know why? Because we are warriors, and warriors fight."
~Unknown

If you have made it this far into the book, we thank you for sticking with us and hope that you have found the information contained in the previous chapters to be both helpful and healing. One of the many goals with this book was always to provide resources for veterans and their families, which is what this entire chapter will be dedicated to achieving. While it is impossible to list every organization, program and professional dedicated to the issue of combat PTSD, we have provided a sampling to get readers headed in the right direction. Our companion website, www.warsendwithme.com also features resources veterans and their families may find useful, so we encourage you to stop by and check it out.

Psychological Services and Counseling Resources

Accepting that behaviors and symptoms may be a sign of PTSD is only half the battle for veterans and active military members. Knowing where to go to seek help and determining the best treatment options can be daunting. Below is a list of organizations, agencies and individuals able to diagnose and treat PTSD. When choosing a therapist or counseling service, the National Center for

PTSD suggests finding a professional who specializes in trauma-related care, as well as someone who practices evidence-based treatments for PTSD, such as cognitive processing therapy, Eye Movement Desensitization and Reprocessing (EMDR) or prolonged exposure therapy. Family doctors also may be able to recommend a local practitioner who accepts the veteran's health insurance and is reputable. Veterans who are eligible to receive services through the VA can request information for VA-provided PTSD counseling and psychological resources.

- American Academy of Child & Adolescent Psychiatry
  https://www.aacap.org
  Provides facts and resources for families with children who may need counseling relating to PTSD. This can be especially useful in locating a child psychiatrist who is capable of helping children of a parent or parents with PTSD to process what is happening.
- American Psychiatric Association
  https://www.psychiatry.org/
  Provides facts and resources for PTSD, as well as a tool to help locate psychiatrists who specialize in combat PTSD.
- American Psychological Association
  http://www.apa.org/
  Provides resources for a number of psychological conditions, as well as a "find a psychologist" tool.
- Anxiety and Depression Association of America
  https://adaa.org/
  Provides information on depression and resources for help ranging from online support groups to in-person treatment for children and adults.
- Association for Behavior and Cognitive Therapies
  http://www.abct.org

Provides a tool for finding a CBT therapist in your area.

- Military One Source

www.militaryonesource.com or toll free at (800) 342-9647

Contracted mental health counselors are available to confidentially speak to veterans or family members and provide information that can help them to deal with difficult situations. Individuals who use this resource can expect to find 24/7, person-to-person help.

- National Alliance on Mental Illness (NAMI)

https://www.nami.org/

This organization provides access to resources, support groups and therapists, including an entire section for combat veterans and active military members.

- PTSD Coach Mobile App

This free app is available for Android devices on the Google Play store and for Apple devices on the iTunes store. It is designed to help veterans learn about and manage the symptoms associated with PTSD.

- PTSD United

http://www.ptsdunited.org/

This nonprofit organization is dedicated to providing support and resources to individuals with PTSD and their families. They provide an awareness and educational component for anyone who wishes to learn more about trauma-related stress disorders. The organization offers an anonymous, online support network called Citizen Zen. It is available 24/7 for individuals living with PTSD to connect with one another to share stories and offer support.

- Soldier's Heart

https://www.soldiersheart.net/

As featured in Chapter 11 of this book, Soldier's Heart is a nonprofit organization offering programs and re-sources designed to transform the emotional, moral and spiritual wounds from war and military service.

Service Dogs and Emotional Support Animals

As discussed earlier in the book, many veterans find service and emotional support dogs to be useful in dealing with everyday living tasks or in coping with emotional needs. The following is a sampling of organizations which provide service dogs to veterans regardless of the location of the veteran. Wait lists to receive a service animal can be long. There are countless other service dog organizations with limited service areas.

*   Canine Companions for Independence
    http://www.cci.org/
    Since 1975, this national organization has helped pair highly-trained service dogs with veterans with disabilities. The service dogs are provided free of charge to qualified veterans.
*   Companions for Heroes
    http://companionsforheroes.org/
    This organization provides rescue dogs that have been trained as service dogs free of charge to veterans with physical disabilities, or those who have been diagnosed with PTSD or a traumatic brain injury. To learn more about the program, or to apply for a service dog, visit their website.
*   Patriot PAWS
    http://patriotpaws.org/
    This organization trains and provides service dogs of the highest quality at no cost to veterans with physical disabilities and those with PTSD.

- This Able Veteran
  http://www.thisableveteran.org/

This service dog organization specifically benefits United States military veterans diagnosed with PTSD. Service dogs trained by the organization provide assistance for veterans dealing with nightmares, depression and social or other anxiety issues as a result of their PTSD. Veterans who would like to be considered for a service dog through this program should visit the This Able Veteran website, where they can obtain an application form. Veterans are required to submit a copy of their DD214 and be under the care of a therapist. Veterans who wish to have a service dog due to disabilities outside of PTSD must have received their injuries as the direct result of their military service.

- Working Dogs for Vets
  https://www.workingdogsforvets.org/

This nonprofit program enables veterans to train their own dog to be a service dog and promotes the rescue of shelter dogs for this purpose. The organization does not charge veterans for this service and is dependent on volunteers to accomplish its mission.

Substance Abuse Resources

Many veterans and active military members dealing with PTSD turn to substance abuse to "self-medicate" if they do not want to accept or seek treatment for their condition. We have included a list of resources which specialize in substance abuse treatment and counseling, including those specializing in substance abuse among veterans.

- American Addiction Centers
  https://americanaddictioncenters.org/

American Addiction Centers provides individuals battling addiction with the high quality treatment that is marked by clinical excellence, individualized care and a supportive community. They have locations across the country and address the underlying cause for the addiction as part of the treatment plan.

- Substance Abuse and Mental Health Services Administration (SAMHSA)
  https://www.samhsa.gov/find-help
  This agency provides mental health-related information, resources and referrals, including a crisis hotline.

Veteran-Focused Resources

The following is a list of groups nationwide whose focus is on serving military families and veterans in a variety of areas. Some provide financial assistance, while others help locating resources for treatment for substance abuse or mental health conditions. Still others are dedicated to helping veterans and their families navigate through the Veterans Administration system to ensure they are receiving all of the benefits and services to which they are entitled.

- American Legion
  https://www.legion.org/
  The American Legion is the nation's largest wartime veterans service organization. Like the VFW, it is able to provide members with resources and advocacy services. To find a legion post near you, visit the website and select the "Find a Post" option at the top of the page.
- Disabled American Veterans
  https://www.dav.org/
  This advocacy organization helps disabled veterans navigate

through the VA system to ensure they are receiving all the benefits and services to which they are entitled. This organization can be extremely helpful to veterans who are fighting to obtain a PTSD diagnosis or receive disability, when appropriate, once they are diagnosed.

- The Battle Continues

  http://thebattlecontinues.org/

  As featured in Chapter 5 of this book, this nonprofit organization is dedicated to raising awareness and providing assistance to veterans returning from war.

- Veterans of Foreign Wars (VFW)

  https://www.vfw.org

  The VFW is more than just a social organization for veterans who have served in overseas conflicts. It also is able to provide veterans with resources and to help advocate on their behalf. Find a local VFW chapter near you using the "Find a Post" option on the main website.

Recommended Reading

This section is a listing of other books and articles about PTSD which we feel may be helpful to veterans or family members wishing to learn more about the clinical or historical side of PTSD. It also contains books by authors mentioned in previous chapters of our book.

- "War and the Soul"

  Author: Dr. Edward Tick

  Publication Date: 2005

  This book is available through booksellers including Amazon and Barnes and Noble. It also is available through the Soldier's Heart website. Many public libraries also carry copies of the book.

- "Warriors Return: Restoring the Soul After War"
  Author: Dr. Edward Tick
  Publication Date: 2014

This book is available through booksellers including Amazon and Barnes and Noble. It also is available through the Soldier's Heart website. Many public libraries also carry copies of the book.

- "Once a Warrior, Always a Warrior: Navigating the Transition from Combat to Home"
  Author: Charles Hoge, M.D.
  Publication Date: 2010

This book is available through booksellers including Amazon and Barnes and Noble. It also is available through the Soldier's Heart website. Many public libraries also carry copies of the book.

- "The Complex PTSD Workbook: A Mind-Body Approach to Regaining Emotional Control and Becoming Whole"
  Author: Jim Knipe, Ph.D.
  Publication Date: 2017

This book is available through booksellers including Amazon and Barnes and Noble. It also is available through the Soldier's Heart website. Many public libraries also carry copies of the book. It further discusses the concept of using cognitive processing therapy, as discussed in Chapter 10 of this book, for the treatment of PTSD.

- "An Archetypal Approach to Treating Combat Post-Traumatic Stress Disorder"
  Author: Dr. Roger Brooke
  Publication Date: 2017

This paper discusses the Jungian approach to processing and effectively treating PTSD in combat veterans. It is available on Academia.com by searching for Dr. Brooke.

- "Healing our Warriors"
  Author: Charlotte Cuthbertson
  Publication Date: 2017, Epoch Times
  Online access to the article can be found here: https://www.theepochtimes.com/healing-our-warriors-sharing-the-burdens-veterans-carry-can-help-bring-peace-to-their-troubled-souls_2191448.html.

- "Psychological Trauma and the Combat Veteran"
  Author: Dr. Roger Brooke
  Publication Date: December 2011
  Online access to this article can be found here: http://rogerbrookephd.com/pdfs/Psych%20trauma%20&%20combat%20veteran%20MOWW.pdf.

About the Author
§

Shari L. Berg has known she wanted to be a writer since she was old enough to hold a pencil in her hand. From poetry to short stories, feature stories and blog posts, Ms. Berg has spent a lifetime crafting her art. She received her Bachelor of Arts degree in Journalism from the University of Pittsburgh in May of 1996. During her college career, Ms. Berg worked in several positions within the student newspaper, including writer, copy editor and lead photographer/photo editor.

Upon graduation, Ms. Berg worked as a professional journalist for several daily newspapers for more than 12 years, including the *Lewistown Sentinel* and the *Butler Eagle*. She also has written for several print and online publications in a freelance capacity.

Ms. Berg is an award-winning writer, having received a Golden Quill Award for Journalism in 1998 for a story on the Ku Klux Klan's visit to Butler County, and another in 2004 for a series of stories written on the topic of domestic violence. Ms. Berg also received the John Fiske McHugh Award for Journalism in 1996, which is given to a Journalism student who shows exemplary work in an advanced reporting course. She received the recognition for a senior research project on the topic of publishing rape victims' names in the media.

Ms. Berg is the owner of The Write Reflection, which provides public relations, marketing, copy writing, website management, graphic design, research and other content-related services. She is the author of the history compilation, *"Pioneer Proud, Celebrating 50 Years of Butler County Community College,"* contracted by Butler County Community College in celebration of its 50th anniversary and published in 2015.

Ms. Berg resides in Pittsburgh, Pa. with her family.

About Patrick Strobel

§

Chief Warrant Officer 3 Patrick Strobel enlisted in the U.S. Army in 1988 upon graduation from High School. He received basic training at Fort Dix in New Jersey before reporting to Aberdeen Proving Ground in Maryland for five months to receive advanced training. Following training, he was stationed in Germany, where he would spend the next five years. In 1991, Strobel served a tour of duty as part of Operation Desert Shield/Storm. He later returned to Germany and then Fort Irwin, Calif., in 1993.

In 1997, Patrick returned to Aberdeen Proving Grounds and, in 1999, he was solicited for warrant officer training, which sent him to Alabama for six weeks of very intensive training. Following training, he ended up back in Fort Irwin and then two years later, was stationed in South Korea. In early 2003, Patrick was sent to Fort Carson, Colo., with the 3rd Armored Cavalry Regiment. Shortly thereafter, Patrick was deployed to Iraq as part of the second Gulf

War. In 2005 and again in 2006, Patrick returned to Iraq and in 2007, finished active duty during a yearlong tour in Afghanistan.

He currently works at the Department of the Army Civilian for the Army Sustainment Command.

He and his wife, Donna, reside in Illinois.

Made in the USA
Coppell, TX
01 March 2020

16388623R00088